Leslie Linsley's
Christmas Ornaments and Stockings

Also by Leslie Linsley

Custom Made
Fabulous Furniture Decorations
Wildcrafts
The Decoupage Workshop
Scrimshaw
Decoupage: A New Look at an Old Craft
Decoupage for Young Crafters
Decoupage on . . .
Army Navy Surplus: A Decorating Source
Photocraft
New Ideas for Old Furniture
The Great Bazaar
Making It Personal with Monograms, Initials and Names
Air Crafts
Million Dollar Projects from the 5 & 10¢ Store

More than 100 designs and full-size patterns for
making very special stockings and ornaments

Leslie Linsley's

Christmas
Ornaments and
Stockings

Design and photography
by Jon Aron

St. Martin's Press
Richard Marek

Grateful acknowledgment goes
to my daughter, Lisa Brunhuber,
for her exacting
work on the needlepoint
and cross-stitch projects.

—Leslie Linsley

This is a St. Martin's/Marek book.

Library of Congress Cataloging in Publication Data

Linsley, Leslie.
  Leslie Linsley's Christmas ornaments & stockings.

  1. Christmas decorations. I. Title. II. Title:
Leslie Linsley's Christmas ornaments and stockings.
III. Title: Christmas ornaments & stockings.
IV. Title: Christmas ornaments and stockings.
TT900.C4L56 1982   745.594'1   82-5585
ISBN 0-312-48131-4   AACR2

Design by Jon Aron

10 9 8 7 6 5 4 3 2 1

First Edition

Contents

Introduction 10

General crafting how-to's 13

Fabrics 13

Enlarging designs and patterns 13

Transferring patterns and details to fabric 13

Cutting out patterns in quantity 14

Sewing in quantity 14

Crafting in quantity 15

Stitch and stuff 16

Pastel butterfly 18

Bird of peace 18

Fat cat 20

Woolly mouse 20

Big bear 24

Piglet 24

Stuffed heart stars 27

Magical mystical stars and moon 30

Ribbon stars 32

Miniature folk pillows 35

Sleepy-time doll stocking 38

Striped stocking 42

Needlepoint 45

Needlepoint ornaments 46

Eight-point stars 49

Babes-in-toyland stocking 51

Babes-in-toyland ornaments 52

Butterfly ornaments   55

Antique cornucopia   57

Felt forum   59

Penguin   61

Contented cat   61

Papa bear   64

Mama bear   64

Teddy pops   66

Circus cat   68

Angel cat   70

Cool cats   72

Folk doll   75

Boys and girls together   81

Not a creature was stirring   82

Elf stocking   86

Paper and wood   89

Paper patchwork stars   90

Country charmers   92

Swingers   105

Trees for the tree   106

Mexican ornaments   108

Embroidery enchantments   112

Twinkle, twinkle, little star stocking   114

Star light, star bright stocking   118

Pet stockings   121

Counted cross-stitch perfection   125

Cross-stitch stars   126

Baby's first stocking   129

Personalized sachet ornaments   132

Stocking for a little angel   135

Prancing reindeer stocking   138

Scandinavian snowflake stocking   141

Initially hearts   144

Christmas soldiers   146

Scrap crafts   149

Granny square jewels   150

Patchwork stocking   152

Buttons and bells   155

Gift tags   158

Crochet   161

Little angel   162

Crochet snowflakes   165

Mouse stocking   168

Reindeer ornament   171

Gingerbread puppets and house   173

Source list   176

Leslie Linsley's
Christmas Ornaments and Stockings

Introduction

"Over the river and through the woods to grandmother's house we go" conjures up an image of Christmastime that hardly any of us can remember. Yet, over the years as the holiday season has become more and more flamboyant and commercialized, the idea of a real old-fashioned Christmas seems very appealing. It is a romantic thought to return to an era of horse-drawn carriages over snow-laden roads, past homes spewing smoke from rooftop chimneys. One can imagine families gathered around a roaring fire stringing popcorn and cranberry garlands for the tree that will be brought in freshly cut from the nearby woods.

In the large country kitchen children roll out floured dough for Christmas cookies and wear white starched aprons over handmade dresses. The sweet smells of cranberry bread seep from the oven and drift through the house.

The table is set with china and crystal that has passed from one generation to the next. A centerpiece of freshly cut evergreens surrounds bayberry-scented candles on the pine table.

In New England where I celebrate Christmas, one can still find the warmth and nostalgia of yesteryear that many of us yearn for from time to time. And many of the traditional family activities that surround the Christmas season are celebrated year after year, generation after generation, unaffected by the commercialism that is more prevalent in our cities. While the cities expose us to an overabundance of things to buy as well as their special kind of holiday romance, small towns everywhere emphasize the materials for making things. Fabric shops, craft stores, art supply departments and notions stores are well stocked during the holidays, bringing us the excitement that comes with the creative process.

Christmas is an excuse for crafting, if one needs an excuse. We are reminded of Christmas crafting early in the summer when the magazines bring out their special issues to give us a head start. In late summer the churches and clubs send announcements reminding everyone to start making things for the Christmas bazaar. And well before the Thanksgiving turkey has been devoured, the crafting materials have been bought for the frantic month ahead.

For many of us who are too busy to consider making gifts, the idea of making something for Christmas is still appealing. Creating the traditional Christmas stockings and ornaments fulfills this need. These projects can be made quickly and simply, or more elaborately if we choose, and the time spent to make them is worthwhile because of their lasting quality.

The idea of bringing out the handmade stockings every year, or dressing the tree with the handmade ornaments, goes along with a desire for continuity in family celebrations. Each year we are adding to the keepsakes that will be passed down to our children and grandchildren.

With more mothers working, the quality of time spent with children is important. Making craft projects together is satisfying for everyone. Children like to feel they have contributed in a meaningful and tangible way. Over the years I have made dozens of Christmas decorations with my children. Now, as young adults, they love to hold up each one and remember when they made it. "Oh, look, I made this when I was in the sixth grade," one of my daughters will say. "And I made this star when I had the chicken pox," Amy will remember. Finding the projects in the Christmas box each year is more fun than hanging them. This makes everyone eager to add to the collection. As teenagers, they still hang the stockings we made together when they were quite young. These traditions will probably be carried on in their own households.

This is a celebration of Christmas through crafting. The book concentrates on designs and patterns for stockings and ornaments because of the vast interest in this area of crafting. Since this is the most popular, it makes sense to show as much variety of techniques and designs as possible. There never seem to be enough new ideas.

Every year there are new trends in decorating, clothing and lifestyles. Crafting is part of these trends. We make accessories for home decorating to go with the latest colors and styles, and our changing tastes affect the designs we choose for crafting projects as well. When it comes to Christmas projects we tend to stick to the traditional, but we do incorporate the changes more than we realize. For example, new fabrics and colors are always being introduced, and it's fun to use them when possible. In response to the renewed interest in American and French country furnishings, we've designed some ornaments that reflect a country flair. The romance of lace, velvet and satin is reflected in others.

All the stockings and ornaments have been designed in a variety of ways so you can interchange them, substitute materials that you might prefer and find the technique that is the most appealing to you. Almost all of the patterns are full-size, and when this wasn't possible (as with some stockings), the pattern is very easy to enlarge. All the decorations are full-size, even when the stocking shape must be enlarged. (See page 13)

Since many of the letters I receive let me know that you want to make gift tags, I've included a section on making gift tags that are simple, quick, easy and utilize the scraps from other projects. These are full-size patterns and reflect the designs throughout the book.

So settle back and browse through the various sections. It's time to make your home special. When you begin crafting, consider a theme. Will it be romantic with satin and lace, or reflect country charm with warm calico, patchwork and dainty prints? Most of the stockings have ornaments that go with them, so you can carry out a theme. Some of the designs can also be adapted for a centerpiece or door decoration.

Taking the time to fill your home with warmth and care will be appreciated by all. When Christmas is over and the ornaments are packed away, you will have a treasury of trimmings to add to next year's joy. Year after year you can create the heirlooms that will make yours a special Christmas celebration.

General crafting how-to's

All the projects in the book are made with a variety of materials and crafting techniques. The materials and directions are listed and explained with each project. However, there are some general tips and how-to's that pertain to all. The following is a summary of that information for easy referral as you work on each project. The general directions are especially helpful when making several ornaments at once. They will tell you the best way to do various steps in quantity.

Fabrics

Almost any fabric can be used for making stockings and ornaments; however, some are easier to work with for different crafting techniques.

Felt is perhaps the best because it won't fray and therefore doesn't have to be hemmed. Muslin is a good inexpensive material for backing stockings and some stuffed ornaments, and is excellent for stenciled designs (see page 28) as it takes the acrylic paint well. Velvet, corduroy and fake furs make fat cats, bunnies and other animal shapes look almost real.

Polished cottons and satin give the stockings and ornaments an elegant look, and small overall prints like calico are good choices for these small projects.

Enlarging designs and patterns

Most of the projects have been designed and presented full-size. However, when a design must be enlarged it will appear in the book with a grid over it, indicating the size each square represents.

For example, one square may equal 1 inch, in which case you will transfer or copy the design to graph paper marked with 1-inch squares. Pads of graph paper are available in art or needlework stores.

Transferring patterns and details to fabric

You can trace most of the designs from the book and transfer them to fabric in the following way. Tape the tracing to a windowpane. Hold the fabric over the tracing and follow the lines.

Another method is to retrace the design on the back of the paper. Place this in position on the fabric and rub the pencil over the design outlines. The design will appear faintly on the fabric. Remove the tracing and go over the outline with a pencil. For dark fabrics, use a dressmaker's carbon and a tracing wheel.

If you cut around the outline of the pattern, you can transfer the details by punching through the tracing paper with a ballpoint pen and making a mark on the fabric. This will tell you where to add embroidery details.

Cutting out patterns in quantity

When making ornaments and sometimes stockings, you will probably be working in multiples. Even if every ornament isn't exactly the same, if you are making a felt ornament, for example, you might want to make several for your tree. Or you may want to create an overall theme of stuffed butterflies. It is more efficient to make several items from one pattern. They can be varied in the fabrics, colors and trimmings.

Use a large enough area to do all your cutting. Take time to study the pattern and determine how you will place it on the fabric to get the most from your material.

Choose the fabrics and lay one on top of the other. The number of layers to be cut at one time will depend on the type of fabric used. If you are using a solid or overall print, you won't have a problem with placement. However, when using stripes or a print that reads only one way, you'll have to be more careful.

Pin all material together and place the pattern on top. After the outline of the pattern is cut, each piece must be individually marked. (See transferring details.)

Sewing in quantity

Plan the steps carefully. If there are several pieces to a pattern, jot down the order in which they will be put together. Plan your thread colors so that all stitching with one color can be done before changing thread. If you are making a batch of felt ornaments, all parts that are the same should be cut and stitched at once, rather than finishing one complete item before going on to the next. If you are making stuffed ornaments, cut and stitch all shapes, then add the stuffing and finally do all hand stitching at one time.

When working on the cross-stitch projects (see page 125), draw the outlines of the star pattern, for example, on the fabric as many times as needed. Cross-stitch each ornament before cutting it out and finishing.

If you are making more than one stocking, cut out the patterns and make all the basic shapes. Assemble your trimmings and design all elements at the same time.

Crafting in quantity

No matter what technique you use, if you are making many of one project, there are shortcuts for the preliminary work. The idea is to do the preparatory steps as efficiently as possible so that you can concentrate on the creative aspects of the project. If you choose the stenciled heart star ornaments (see page 28), for example, you will do all stenciling before cutting out the individual star shapes so that the paint can be used, put away and then the cutting and stitching can be done as efficiently.

The Mexican stars (see page 108) made from clothespins provide another example. First, all pins are taken apart; then each group is spray-painted a different color before assembling the pieces. This project would be impractical if not made in quantity, and because so many different paints are used, it would be expensive to make just one.

Some projects have to be done individually and would take too long to make in quantity. Some of the needlepoint projects are one-of-a-kind. When choosing which projects you want to make, keep in mind how you want to use them and which you feel lend themselves to crafting in quantity.

Stitch and stuff

Stuffed ornaments in a variety of shapes, colors and patterns are easy and fun to make. It is especially nice when your tree is covered with delightful shapes made with the same feeling. For example, a tree covered with butterflies made from pastel polished cotton prints or barnyard animals in calico or polka dots. These soft three-dimensional ornaments have a wonderful handmade quality that will give your tree a one-of-a-kind personality.

The shapes have been designed for easy cutting and stitching in one piece. This makes it possible to cut several at one time, stitch all and finally stuff. Very little detail work is required. However, you can add decorative trims to make the ornaments more elaborate. As you will notice, the section of animal heads presents one basic shape for the bear, pig and cat, making it possible to cut them all out at the same time. However, the faces are what distinguish one from the other, giving each the specific characteristics for that animal.

The selection of material is the important part here. If you select prints, the patterns should be small and overall. If you choose solids, think about using texture like velvet, satin, wool. Add lace around a velvet butterfly, for example, or jeweled wings of sequins.

For portability, you can make these by hand rather than machine and perhaps add some embroidery to solid fabrics.

Silver and gold metallic and nylon materials are excellent for glittery Christmas tree ornaments. Simple shapes of stars and half-moons become exotic with no added trimmings needed.

When stuffing ornaments, the filling you use makes a difference in the finished item. A polyester fiberfill is the most popular. If you are quilting, a polyester or cotton batting is easy to work with. To make smooth, rounded, stuffed ornaments, consider backing the front and back pieces of fabric with a piece of batting before stitching, turning and stuffing until full.

Basic sewing and stuffing directions: The following projects are made from easy-to-get, easy-to-work-with cotton prints. Most of the ornaments can be made from scraps of material because so little is needed.

The basic sewing directions for each of the stuffed ornaments are the same. The animal critters have simple painted faces. For these you will need a variety of acrylic paint tubes, and a crochet hook or knitting needle will help to get stuffing into small areas like ears. Under each project you will find a list of materials that includes paint colors and specific directions pertaining to that project.

Trace and transfer the shape and specific facial details to the fabric. Each project has fabric suggestions for the specific animal.

16

Cut 2 pieces for each ornament. Stitch details on one piece for the face only where indicated. With right sides together, stitch around the outline, leaving a ¼-inch seam allowance and 2 inches open at bottom edge. Clip at either side of pointed ears or around curved areas and turn right side out. Press.

Fill with loose stuffing and slip-stitch opening. Use a pointed brush to fill in the facial details as indicated with each project.

Making in quantity: To make any of these projects in quantity, trace the pattern and transfer to cardboard. Cut this out to use as a template. Plan how many you'll want from each piece of fabric and trace around the template on the material. Cut a double thickness for each ornament and proceed as per directions. You'll be surprised at how different each one can look by changing the fabric. Some can be light, others dark, and you will change the paint on the faces for each one as well.

Pastel butterfly

An overall floral print in polished cotton was used for the butterflies. I found sample remnants of the print, which is a Schumacher material and comes in several colors. Each butterfly shape is cut from a different color and from a different section of the print. While the overall feeling is similar in fabric texture and design style, each ornament is unique.

Materials: small piece of printed fabric, scrap of black felt, stuffing, 6 strands black embroidery floss, glue.

Directions: Trace, cut, sew and stuff each ornament according to the basic directions in the introduction to this section. Tack down the center between the wings.

Trace the center of the butterfuly on plain white paper and cut out the pattern. Pin the paper to a scrap of black felt and cut this out. Cut out 2 narrow pieces for the antennae.

Glue or stitch the felt body between the wings. Turn this over and glue each tendril to the underside of the head. Tack a 3-inch loop of embroidery floss to the underside of the body and hang.

Bird of peace

Materials: brightly colored cotton fabric, small button or rhinestone, black embroidery floss, scrap of felt (optional), glue.

Directions: Follow basic directions for making body of the bird. Stitch the outline of the wing on the body with embroidery floss or stitch on the machine. Glue a triangle of black felt to front and back of the beak.

This project can be made with felt rather than a print if desired. Cut each piece from a different color felt. Make the body yellow, the wing orange and the tail green.

Add a rhinestone or button for the eye and a loop of embroidery thread for hanging.

Fat cat

Materials: printed cotton fabric; black embroidery floss; loose polyfill; yellow, black, light gray (a drop of black mixed with white) acrylic paint; pointed artist's brush; 3 pieces of 6-inch-long stem wire; 6 inches ¼-inch yellow ribbon; bell.

Directions: Make the basic shape using the general directions in the introduction. To create the face, paint the almond-shaped eye with a bright yellow. Fill in eyeball area with black. The nose is light gray, and the mouth is stitched with a running or stem stitch of yellow or black embroidery floss, depending on the background color of your fabric.

Paint the wire stem black. When dry, insert each one as indicated on the pattern. Each one should pass through the fabric so the whiskers are 2 inches long on each side of the face, with 2 inches inside the fabric. Attach bell, bow and hanging loop.

Woolly mouse

Materials: gray printed cotton, gray wool or felt, loose polyfill, black embroidery floss, 8 pieces of 5-inch-long stem wire, white and black paint, pointed artist's brush.

Directions: Once the outline of the pattern is traced, stitch around the head where the ears are attached. If you are using gray felt, you can add a smaller piece of pink felt cut to fit inside the ears. Proceed with the basic directions from the introduction.

The face can be created with small pieces of felt, or paint eyes white and eyeball black. Fill nose area with black paint.

Paint the stem wire black. When dry, insert each one into the fabric on one side of the face where indicated on the pattern. Push through to the other side so there is 1 inch of fabric over the nose covering the wire. Adjust wire so the whiskers are of equal length on each side and bend slightly downward (whiskers optional).

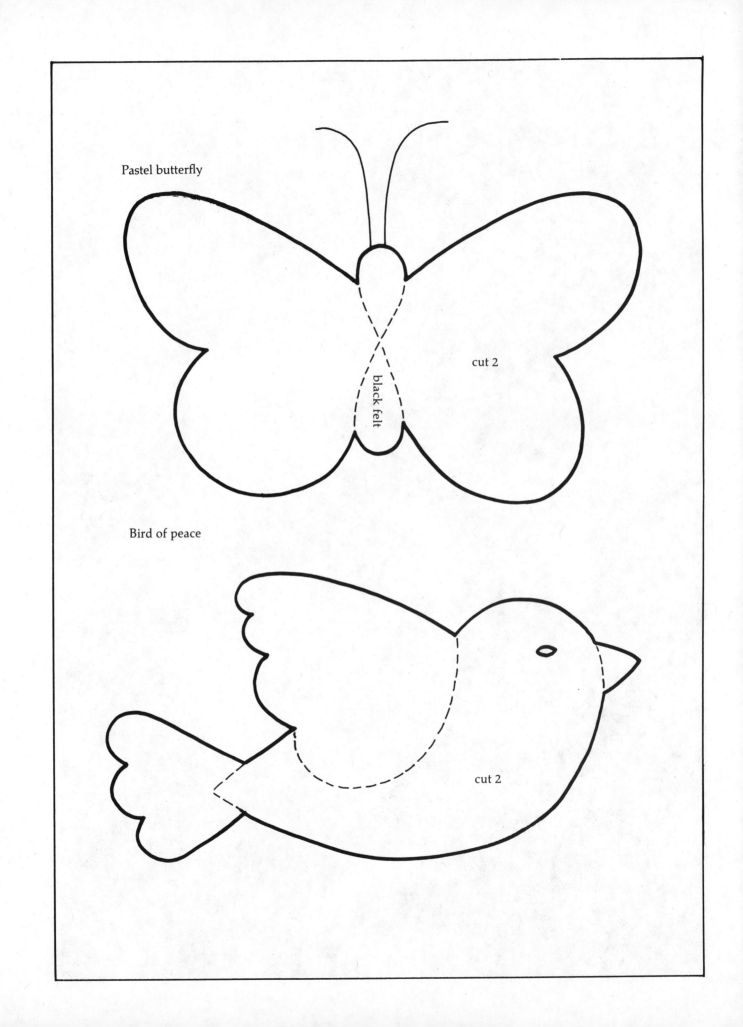

Pastel butterfly

black felt

cut 2

Bird of peace

cut 2

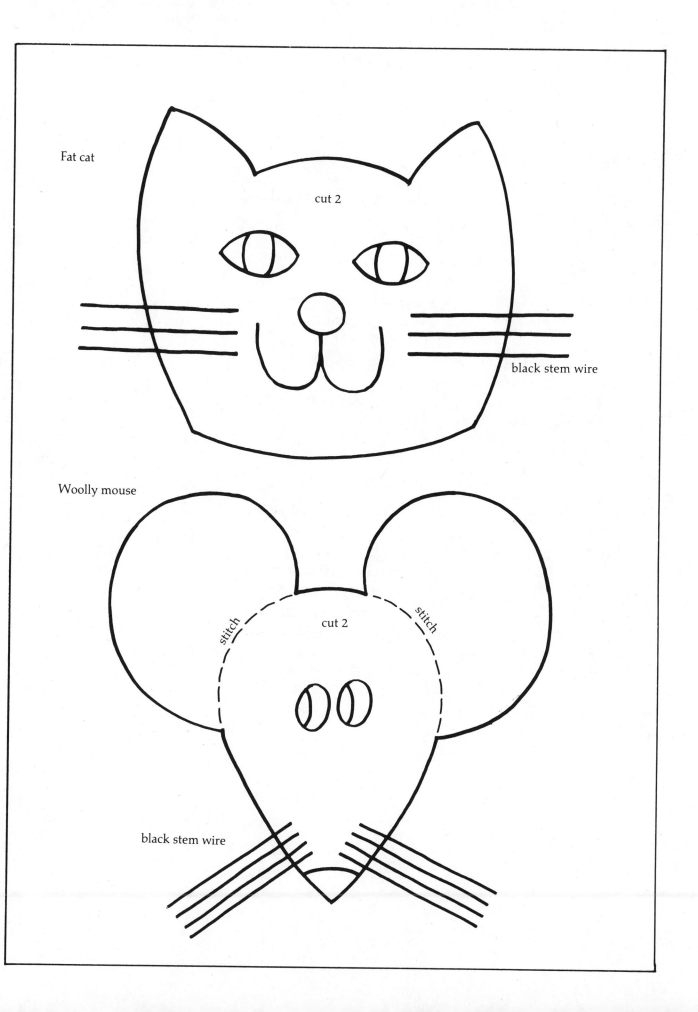

Fat cat

cut 2

black stem wire

Woolly mouse

stitch

cut 2

stitch

black stem wire

Big bear

Materials: printed fabric (not too dark, so painted face will show); small pointed artist's brush; brown, white and blue acrylic paint; loose polyfill; black embroidery floss; small piece of ¼-inch blue ribbon; bell.
Directions: Trace and transfer the shape and face details to the fabric. See general directions in introduction for cutting and sewing the shape.

With a pointed brush fill in the nose area with dark brown acrylic paint, the ears with cream color (a drop of brown added to white) and the circle of eyes with blue. Add black to the center of each eye. Add the mouth with brown paint or with a running or back stitch of black embroidery floss. (See stitch guide page 44.)

Make a little bow tie and tack it with a small bell under his chin. Attach a 3-inch loop of embroidery floss for hanging.

Piglet

Materials: small piece of pink printed or solid fabric; small pointed artist's brush; green, red and white acrylic paint; loose polyfill; red embroidery floss; small piece of ¼-inch green ribbon; bell (optional).
Directions: Trace and transfer the shape and face details to the fabric. See general direction in introduction for assembling piglet head.

Use the artist's brush to fill in green paint for the eyes, with white eyeballs. Add a drop of white paint to red and paint snout. Add 2 dots of red on the nose where indicated on pattern.

Make a small bow and tack with the bell to the bottom of the ornament. Add a strand of red embroidery floss for hanging. For added detail you can embroider around snout with 3 strands of red floss.

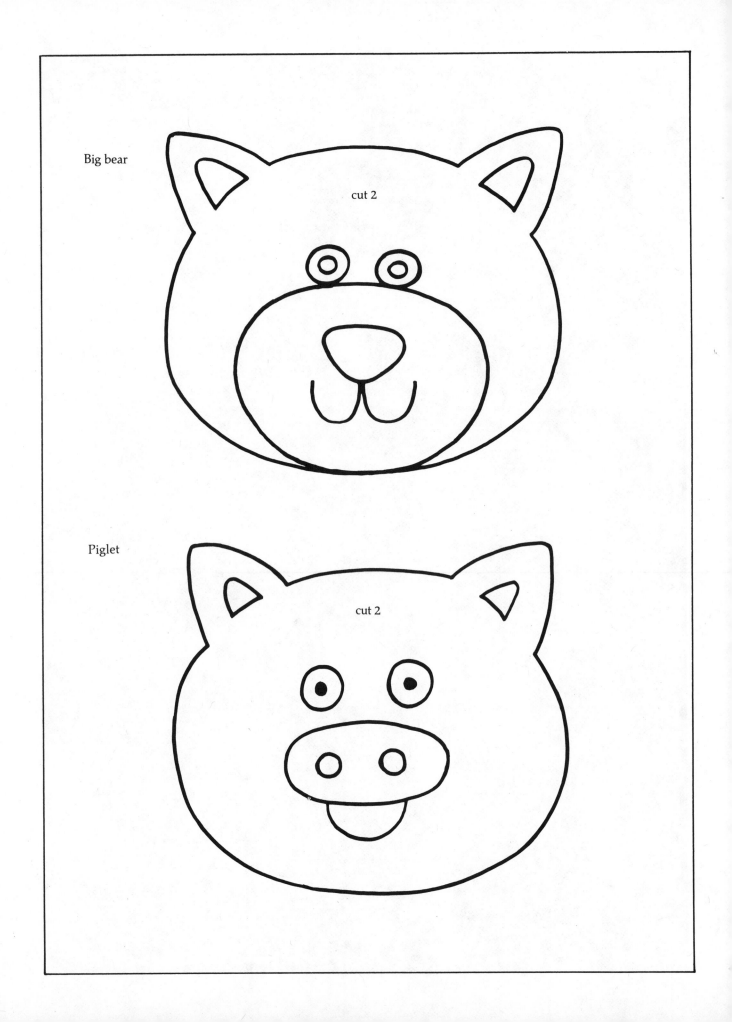

Big bear

cut 2

Piglet

cut 2

Stuffed heart stars

This basic eight-point star is made of inexpensive unbleached muslin. The heart decoration is stenciled with acrylic paint. This project is easiest and more practical when made in multiples rather than one. The muslin accepts the paint without bleeding and the color is bright. Imagine an entire tree filled with these cheerful star ornaments. Or make a dozen to fill the branches of a little table tree to set in a hallway. Children will enjoy helping with this project, as you will see there are two or three steps they can do themselves.

Materials: 1 yard of muslin yields 18 ornaments, stencil paper (art store), stencil brush, red and green acrylic paint, polyester fill, embroidery floss or ¼-inch satin ribbon for hanging, needle and thread, pencil, scissors, craft knife such as X-Acto.

Directions: Fold fabric in half so you have a double thickness. Trace the star pattern, which is shown actual size, and transfer to the fabric as many times as the number of ornaments you wish to make.

Trace the heart pattern and transfer to the stencil paper. Cut out each heart. Transfer the star pattern to the stencil paper so that the heart cutouts are in position within the outline. Cut out this star. This is the pattern for stenciling each star.

Stenciling: Squirt a small amount of green acrylic paint into a shallow dish or onto a shirt cardboard. Hold the stencil brush in an upright position. The brush should be dry, and the paint is applied to the cutout areas with a tapping motion. Begin by tapping off excess paint before filling in the cutout hearts. The center hearts are green and the outer ones are red. When the stencil paper is removed, the design is accurately in position on the fabric. Wait for the paint to dry.

Cut out 2 fabric stars for each ornament. Pin right sides together and stitch around edges, leaving an opening for stuffing. Turn right side out. Press from the back.

Fill the star with polyester fill, using a pointed object (a crochet hook is perfect for this) to get the filling into each point. Stitch opening closed and attach a loop of red embroidery floss or ribbon for hanging.

To make in quantity: If you are making a dozen or more ornaments, trace and transfer the design to the stencil paper. This will include the stitch line as well as the cutting line for the star. Cut out the star. Use your craft knife to cut out each heart. Cut a line through the stencil paper for each sewing line. Use this pattern as a template and draw around the outside with a soft pencil on your fabric. Make pencil lines for the stitching as well. In this way each time you place the stencil of the star pattern on the fabric, the area to be stenciled will be in register.

You will begin by stenciling one circle of hearts in one color on all stars. Then begin again with the first star and stencil the circle of hearts with the next color. All ornaments will have a stenciled design before doing all cutting and stitching.

Stuffed heart star

Use this pattern for both cutting fabric and stencil.

Magical mystical stars and moon

Cover your entire tree with stars and moons encircled in clouds. It's so easy to make these brightly colored felt stars in different sizes. The largest will encircle the bottom of the tree and gradually get smaller toward the top.

Materials: a number of felt squares in a variety of colors, polyester fiberfill fat batting, thread to match felt.

Directions: The patterns are given full-size. Trace each size on plain paper and cut out to use as a template. Outline the star on felt colors as many times as desired. Do not cut out.

Sandwich a piece of batting between 1 layer of felt and the felt with a star outline on top. Pin together. Machine-stitch through all 3 layers just inside the pencil line. Cut out each felt layer of the star separately at the pencil line. Do not cut through the batting. Gently pull away the batting so there is an outline of fluff around every point on the star. Attach a loop of embroidery floss to match each star and hang.

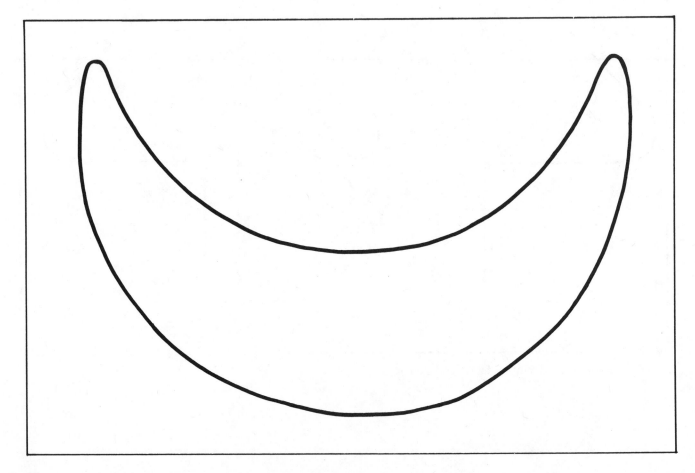

Ribbon stars

Make a batch of ribbon stars from the scraps left over from your ribbon stockings. (See page 155.) They can be as gay as you want, combining a variety of colors, designs and patterns. Or choose a color combination of red and green or pastels and make all the stars match. Ribbon comes in stripes and dots as well, for another variation. Use whatever ribbons you use on the ornaments for all your packages too. This will give you an interesting theme and will solve all your decorating problems.

Materials: small piece of muslin, small piece of felt, several strips of multicolored ½-inch ribbon, scissors, pins, polyfill, needle and thread.

Directions: Trace the star pattern and transfer it to the muslin. Place this over the felt and cut out 2 stars.

Pin strips of ribbon across the front of the muslin star. Stitch along each edge. If you prefer, you can cut a piece of fusible web from the

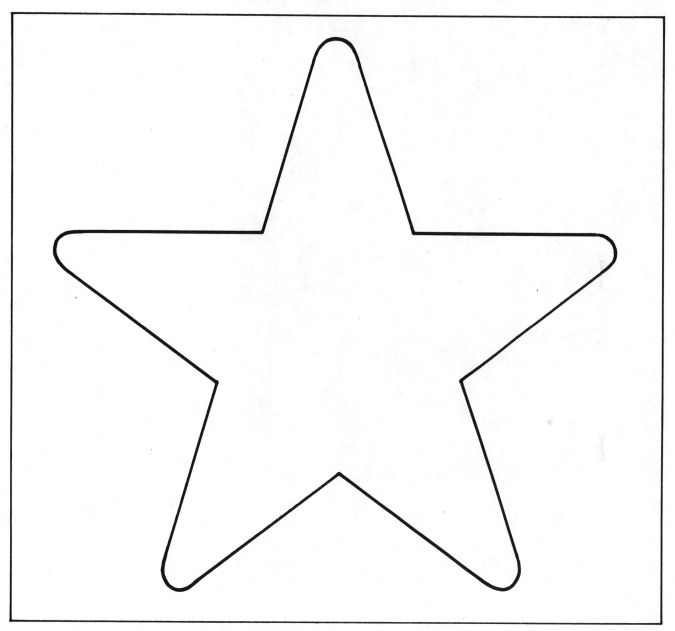

Use this pattern for magical mystical stars and ribbon stars

star pattern. Place this between the muslin and ribbons and iron in place. No stitching necessary.

Place the felt star on top of the ribbon star and stitch around the edges, leaving an opening for turning. Clip around each star point.

Turn the star right side out and press. Stuff with polyfill until the star is very full. Use a pointed object to push the stuffing into each point. A blunt pencil or crochet hook is good for this purpose. Slip-stitch the opening and add a piece of string, yarn or ribbon for hanging.

Making in quantity: You can easily make a wide variety of these ornaments by first creating your ribbon fabric from all the odds and ends of ribbon you can find. Simply sew strips of ribbon to the muslin until you have enough material from which you can cut the number of stars desired.

Make a template of cardboard for the star pattern. Place this on the back of the ribbon-covered muslin and draw around it with a soft pencil as many times as needed. Pin this to a piece of felt the same size, and cut out all stars before sewing together as above.

Miniature folk pillows

Traditional patchwork designs can be used for a country motif in ornaments. However, they are not done in traditional patchwork technique. Here, we have avoided the cutting, folding and stitching of little fabric pieces in favor of fabric crayon transfer. It's as easy as coloring in a child's crayon book, and the quilted outline accents each element of the design. No one would guess that they weren't hand-painted. If you have a small neat crayon fancier in the family, this is the perfect project to make together.

Materials: 1 package Crayola Craft fabric crayons (five-and ten or fabric shops), white cotton fabric, eyelet trim, cording, iron, newspaper, white bond paper, loose polyfill, quilt batting, masking tape, 6 inches ¼-inch satin ribbon.

Directions: Using bond paper, trace a design which is shown actual size. Place this on several layers of newspaper and crayon each area as indicated on the pattern. Make as many colored designs as needed. You can use only one per ornament without recoloring.

Cut 2 pieces of white cotton 4x4 inches and a piece of quilt batting slightly smaller. Turn all edges ¼ inch and press to inside.

Pad your ironing board with several layers of newspaper. Set iron for dry cotton setting. Place 1 piece of cotton face up and tape at the very edge of each corner on the newspaper.

Lay the crayon design facedown in position on the fabric and tape at each corner. Press the iron down firmly on the back of the paper and hold for 3 to 5 seconds. Do this over the entire design.

To check if transfer has "taken," carefully lift one corner and peel back. If the design is too light, hold the iron over the area for a little longer. Untape and lift the paper from the fabric. Do not iron over the design.

With face up, pin the design to the quilt batting and stitch around all design lines. This is optional but adds a nice touch.

Place the cording and eyelet trim between the edges of front and back cotton pieces and stitch around 3 sides. Stuff with loose polyfill. Fold ribbon in half lengthwise and insert the ends in one corner of the open end. Slip-stitch closed.

Making in quantity: Four designs are provided here. They are familiar folk quilt designs and were chosen because they go well together. Decide how many of each you will make and cut twice as many cotton squares.

Divide up the designs and have each member of the family trace and color each one on a separate piece of paper.

When iron is hot enough, transfer all designs to cotton and proceed with each step for all the ornaments. The children will enjoy stuffing each one, and as this is done, you can stitch them up in a jiffy.

Miniature folk pillow designs

Sleepy-time doll stocking

This quilted patchwork stocking is made with scraps of delicate country prints. The front of the stocking looks like the doll's bed. What small child wouldn't be thrilled to find that this tiny doll actually comes out to play? The night before Christmas your child can tuck her doll into bed to wait for Santa's arrival.

Materials: 1 white and 1 pink felt square, 31 printed fabric squares 1½ inches, small piece black and red embroidery floss, polyester batting, 7x9½-inch piece of white cotton, 5 inches white eyelet, 5 inches ⅛-inch pink satin ribbon, pink cotton double-fold bias tape. *For doll:* scraps of light pink, dark pink, cream and black felt; brown yarn; ⅛-inch pink satin ribbon; batting; glue.

Directions: All seams are ¼ inch, which you will add when cutting out the pattern. Use this pattern to cut 2 pieces from pink felt. Cut 1 piece of white felt 4x5½ inches. Cut 1 piece of batting 6½x6½ inches.

Arrange and stitch the patchwork squares in vertical rows as follows: 1 row of 3 squares, 2 rows of 4 squares, 4 rows of 5 squares. Place the piece of batting over the 7x9½-inch piece of cotton with the extra 3½ inches of cotton at the top. Pin at the edges. Place the row of 5 squares face up on the batting 1½ inches in from the heel edge. Place another row of 5 squares face down on the first strip, matching squares.

Stitch inside edge through all layers. Open flat and follow procedure with the remaining strips. Cover the heel side with the strip of 4 squares and the strip of 3 squares. Use the felt pattern to trim all edges.

Turn the edge of the cotton down ¼ inch and fold down to cover the raw edge of the quilt. Press. Position the eyelet under the edge of the sheet with a border of ⅛-inch pink ribbon on top of the edge. Stitch across through all layers of material.

Transfer the cat design to white felt and cut out. Pin to the front of the patchwork area where indicated on the drawing. Stitch around out-lines with black thread.

Cut a piece of batting 3x4½ inches and place this on the top portion of 1 pink felt stocking piece. Pin 4x5½-inch piece of white felt on top so top edges of felt match. Stitch across the bottom edge of the white square.

Place quilted piece on top of pink and white felt piece with heel and toe matching. Pin this face down to the remaining pink felt backing and stitch around outer edge. Leave top open. Trim seams clip at curves and turn to right sides. Turn top edge in ¼ inch and stitch. Bind raw edges with bias tape. Make a hanger for the stocking from 6 inches of bias tape folded in half and stitch. Attach inside stocking.

To make doll: Trace doll pattern on cream-colored felt. Place batting

between this and another piece of cream felt, and stitch around the outline. Cut out.

Trace dress pattern on light pink felt. Cut 2. Cut 2 dark pink pieces for the collar. Stitch front and back of dress together and glue neck pieces to top of dress at front and back. Add a small pocket and eyelet trim to bottom edge. Put dress on doll.

Cut 6 strands of brown yarn 10 inches long. Find the center of the yarn and tack to the top of the doll's head. Tack at each side and braid the strands on either side. Tie ends with yarn or satin ribbons. Cut and glue small black felt shoes on feet.

Use 3 strands of black embroidery floss to fill in the eyes and 3 strands of red for the mouth. Insert doll into pocket on front of stocking.

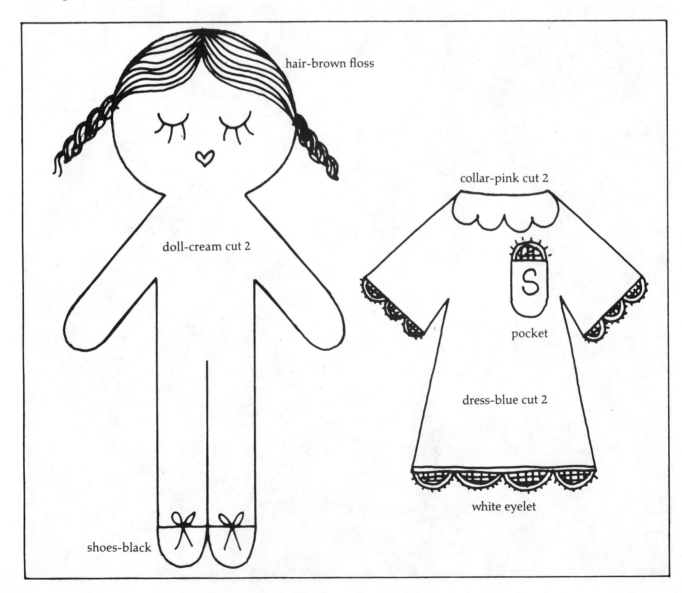

hair-brown floss

collar-pink cut 2

doll-cream cut 2

pocket

dress-blue cut 2

white eyelet

shoes-black

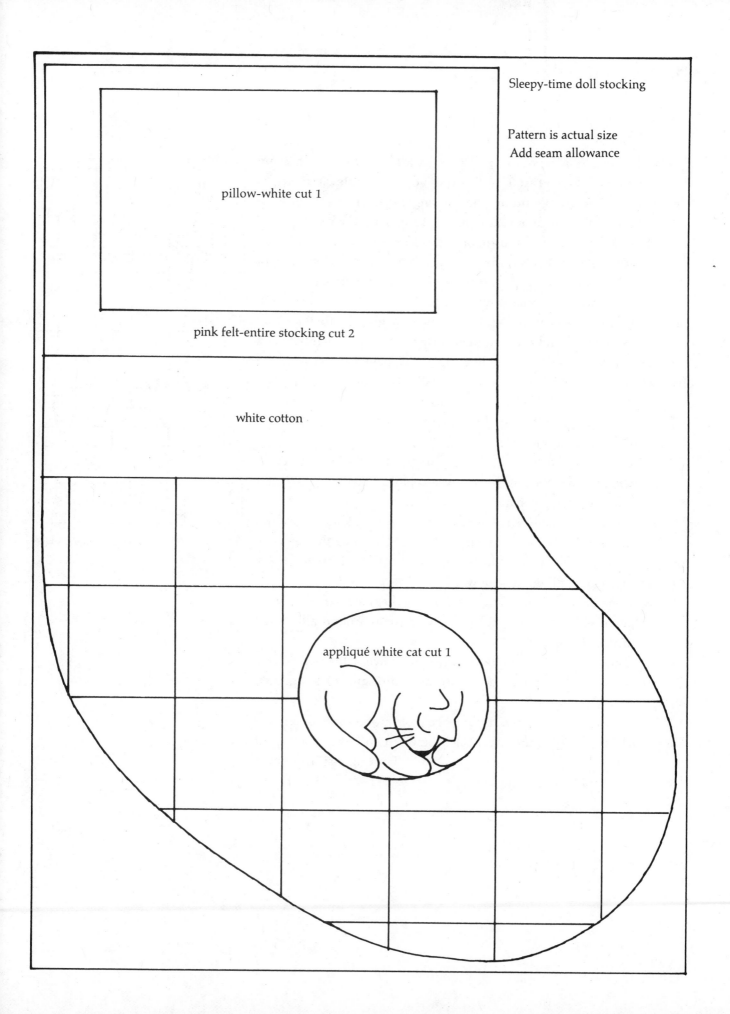

Sleepy-time doll stocking

Pattern is actual size
Add seam allowance

pillow-white cut 1

pink felt-entire stocking cut 2

white cotton

appliqué white cat cut 1

Striped stocking

This stocking is inexpensive and easy to make with iron-on seam binding (Wm. E. Wright Co.). In this way you can create satin stripes without the difficulty of cutting and binding edges or the expense of using ribbons. A package of seam binding contains 3 yards.

Materials: ½ yard bleached muslin or white polyester cotton; quilt batting; 2 packages bright green iron-on seam binding, 1 package bright red; ¼ yard red taffeta; 6 inches ½-inch-wide red satin ribbon.

Directions: Enlarge the pattern (see page 13) and transfer to muslin. Do not cut out. Each green stripe is followed by ⅛-inch space, then a stripe of red, ⅛-inch space and another green stripe. There is 1 inch between a set of stripes. Place seam binding along the penciled lines on the pattern and pin at each end. Iron in position as you go along. The stripes don't have to be cut accurately as you apply them. They can overlap the stocking outline as this pattern will be cut out when covered with stripes. It is a guide for now.

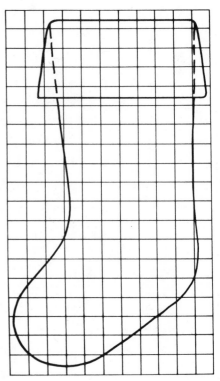

Each square equals 1 inch

Transfer the pattern to another piece of muslin. Use this to cut 4 pieces, including the stocking piece covered with seam binding. Cut 2 pieces of batting slightly smaller.

Sandwich batting between 2 pieces of muslin and stitch around edges. If you want to create a quilted stocking, stitch along the top edge of the first green stripe and the bottom of the second green stripe. Continue to do this all the way down.

Place front and back with right sides together and stitch around outer edge, leaving top open. Trim seams and clip around all curved edges. Turn right side out.

Enlarge and transfer cuff pattern, which is shown actual size. Place on fold of fabric and cut out 2 *double* layers. With right sides together, stitch at each side.

Slip inside stocking and pin to top edge. Fold ribbon in half lengthwise to make a hanging loop and catch between cuff and stocking at the seam line. Stitch ½ inch from top raw edge. Turn right side out over the top to the front of stocking.

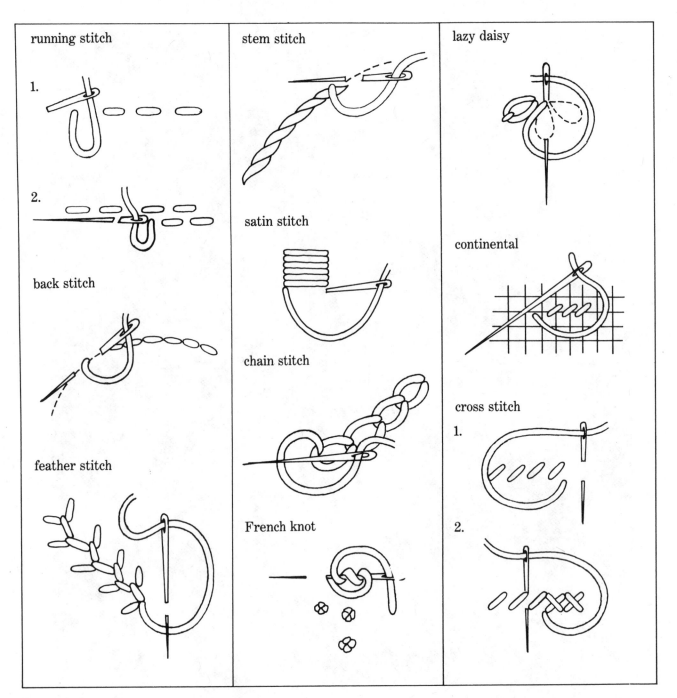

running stitch

1.

2.

back stitch

feather stitch

stem stitch

satin stitch

chain stitch

French knot

lazy daisy

continental

cross stitch

1.

2.

Basic stitches

44

Needlepoint

The needlepoint projects have been designed simply so they can be worked quickly in time for Christmas. The ornaments are done on plastic canvas and are often cut into the shapes of stars, butterflies, or other decorations. When working with plastic canvas, however, it should be stitched before it is cut. Plastic canvas comes in sheets or prepackaged in shapes like round, square and diamond. It is available in three different sizes: five mesh, seven mesh, and ten mesh. The seven mesh can also be found in sheets that measure 11x14-inches as well as shapes. The advantages of this canvas are that no blocking is necessary, it does away with frayed edges, and it can be made into three-dimensional objects. Unlike fabric canvas, plastic canvas is stiff yet flexible. Colored canvas is especially good for Christmas projects as it comes in red and green, so you can do a design without having to fill in the background.

All the projects have been done with easy-to-find Persian-type yarn. It is inexpensive and available in all colors. The skeins are small, so you don't have to buy large amounts of one color. Use yarn strands 18- to 24-inches long. Stitch the designs first and then fill in the background. All projects shown here are worked with the popular Continental stitch. The projects are charted for placement of stitches and each color is indicated on the chart.

An embroidery needle has a blunt point in various sizes. The lower number of a needle is generally used with the lower canvas numbers. For example, a #17–18 needle is used on a #10 mesh. It is helpful to have a good pair of small scissors for clipping ends as you work. If you mask the edges of canvas with tape, it will keep the canvas from raveling as you handle it. A thimble is another helpful tool.

Finishing: When working with a plastic canvas leave at least one row of unworked canvas around the design when cutting. In this way you can bind around the design for a finished edge. Hems and seam allowances are not necessary. If the yarn you are using is thin, use a double strand to completely cover the edges.

Needlepoint ornaments

These little ornaments represent simple, familiar shapes in needlepoint. They are worked in the Continental stitch on 6 count plastic mesh, which you can buy in white, red, green, light blue and other basic colors. The plastic mesh comes in sheets that are easy to cut with a sharp scissors.

Make each of the ornaments in a different color. The early American house design looks especially nice in muted colors like burnt orange, warm gray and earthy green on white mesh. Each ornament will take less than 1 skein of 12½ yard pull yarn. After Christmas, these little beauties can be used as coasters.

Follow the chart for count and colors. Each ornament will take about fifteen minutes.

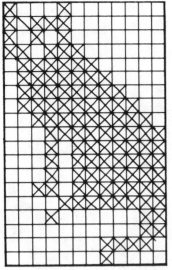

Cat: yellow on green

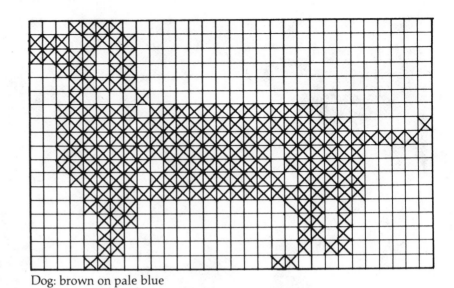

Dog: brown on pale blue

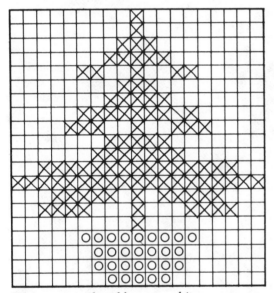

Tree: green with red base on white

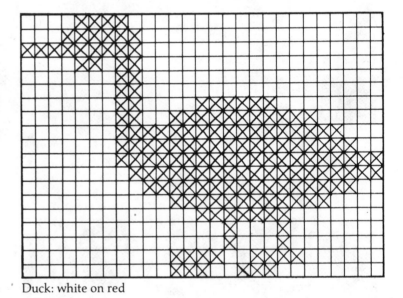

Duck: white on red

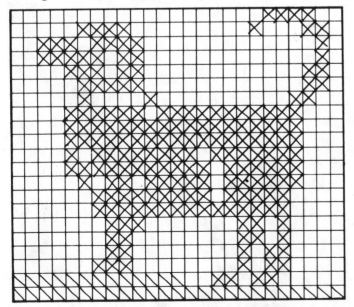

Dog: dark brown; grass: green on pale blue

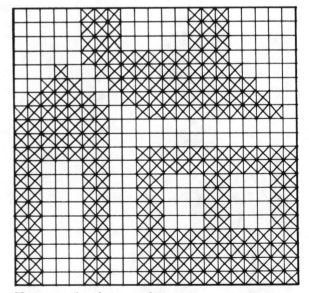

House: earth colors on white

Eight-point stars

The designs for these needlepoint ornaments are deliberately simple, so you can make several to fill the tree. These traditional patchwork star designs are silhouetted. The shapes are cut after they have been stitched. If you repeat one design over and over it is easiest, and you can add variety to your tree by making each one a different color.

The Continental stitch is used for all projects on a #10-count plastic canvas. Bernat 1–2–3-ply Persian-type yarn is used throughout. The colors are indicated on the charted diagram.

Materials: 1 sheet or package of #10-count plastic mesh (five-and-ten or needlework stores), red and white yarn (each ornament takes less than ½ skein), needle.

Directions: There are 4 different early American folk designs. One incorporates an initial, so you can personalize an ornament for each member of your family. Follow the chart for each design and use the alphabet on page 134.

When finished, carefully cut out the star shape and bind the edges. Attach a loop of yarn at the top for hanging.

This choice of tree style is a wonderful way to create a warm, traditional Christmas environment.

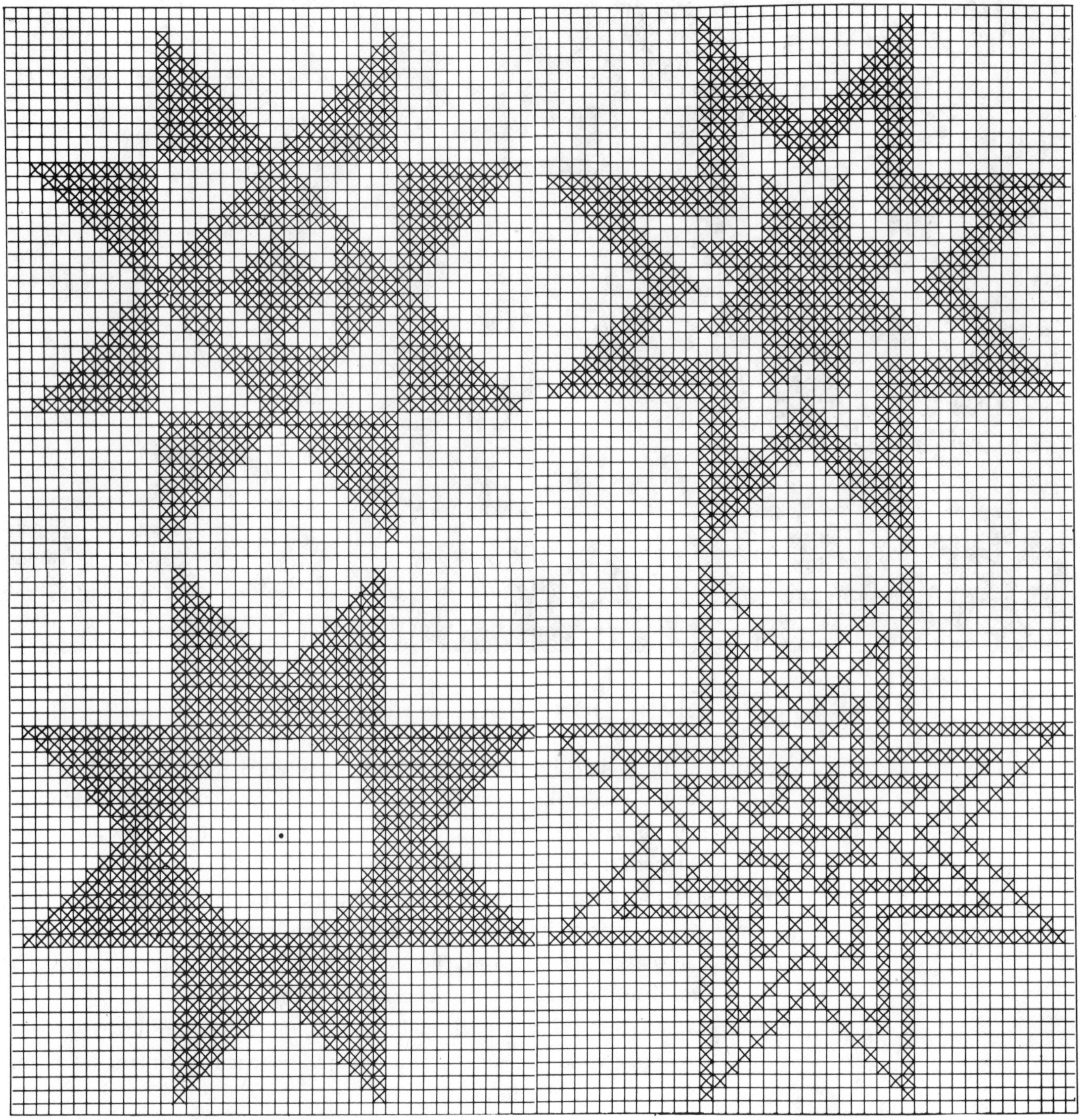

Babes-in-toyland stocking

This needlepoint stocking was designed for a boy or girl, as well as an adult who is young at heart. The Continental stitch is used throughout to create the Alpine design.

A needlepoint stocking is very special. The time and effort put into such projects are well worth the results, which will last forever. Such projects are used year after year and often pass from one generation to another, always a reminder of the loving care that someone put into them.

The pattern for the finished stocking will be 11 inches long.

Materials: 11x14-inch #10-count canvas; Bernat 1–2–3-ply Persian-type yarn 12½-yard pull skeins (2 skeins bright blue, 2 bright green, 1½ red, 1 white and ½ bright yellow); needle; masking tape; 2 pieces 9x12-inch royal blue felt.

Directions: Tape the edges of the canvas to avoid raveling. Enlarge the design and trace it onto the canvas. Follow the charted diagram for placement of stitches. Work across each row until the front of the stocking is filled in. If the canvas needs blocking, steam it and pull into position. Pin to a wooden board to dry. Cut out the stocking with ¼ inch all around. Use the stocking and trace outline on 1 piece of felt. Cut out 2 blue felt stocking pieces. Pin the 2 felt pieces together, matching edges. Machine-stitch around edge, leaving top open. Clip into curves and turn.

Turn the edge of the needlepoint canvas under ¼ inch all around and pin to one layer of felt. Stitch together at edges. Attach a ribbon loop to top corner and hang.

Babes-in-toyland ornaments

The soldier and pony ornaments use the same designs as the Babes-in-toyland stocking. They are worked on 7 count plastic canvas in the same colors as the designs on the stocking. Bind the edges with a contrasting yarn. The pony has a white binding and the soldier's binding is green. Using designs for various decorations is an easy way to coordinate your Christmas look.

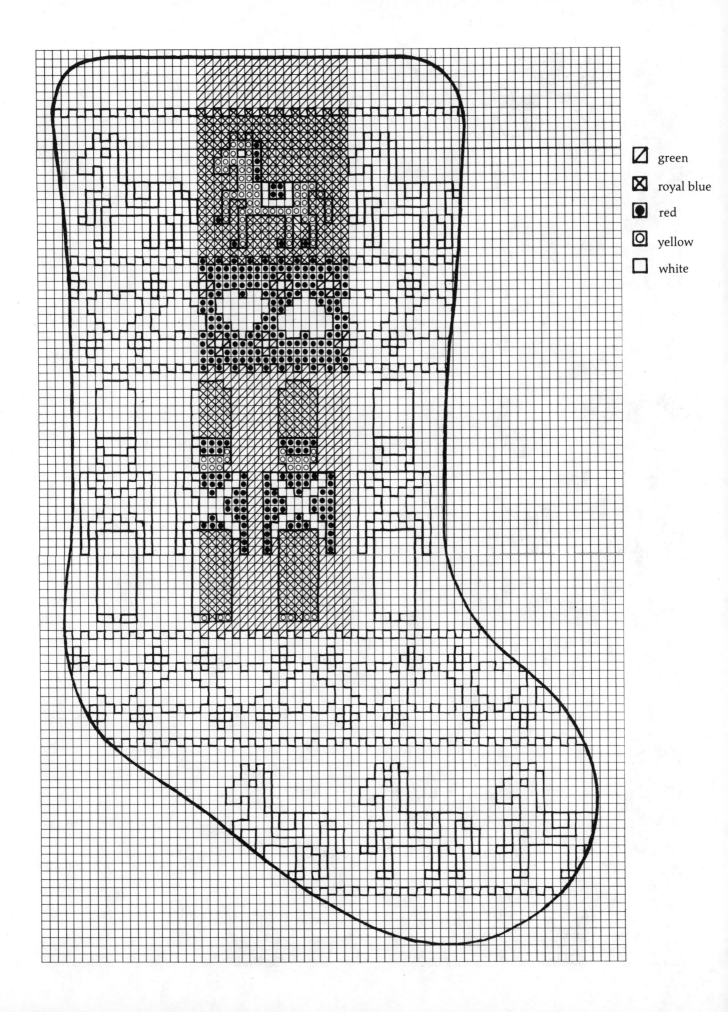

green

royal blue

red

yellow

white

Butterfly ornaments

The butterflies are made in the same way as the star needlepoint ornaments. (See page 49.) Each is stitched on #10-count plastic mesh, and the shape is cut out after the design is complete. Scraps of yarn can be used for this multicolored design. Simply follow the chart for color placement, and work with the Continental stitch.

After the design is finished cut around it, making sure to leave a row of unworked canvas all around. It will be difficult to cut curves and you might find it easier to make straight cuts squaring off these areas. Use a double strand of black yarn to outline the butterflies. As you bind or overcast-stitch around the design the edges will appear rounded to conform to the shape of the butterfly.

These ornaments will work up quickly, so you can cover a tree with them or use them as gift tags for special presents.

★	orange
✿	yellow gold
✕	black
╱	red
▼	rose
■	gray
□	white
▽	pale blue
○	light apple green
·	lavender
●	royal blue

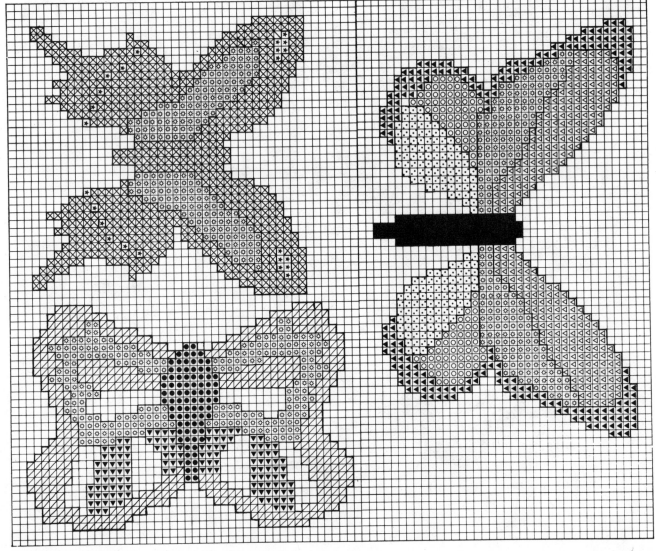

Antique cornucopia

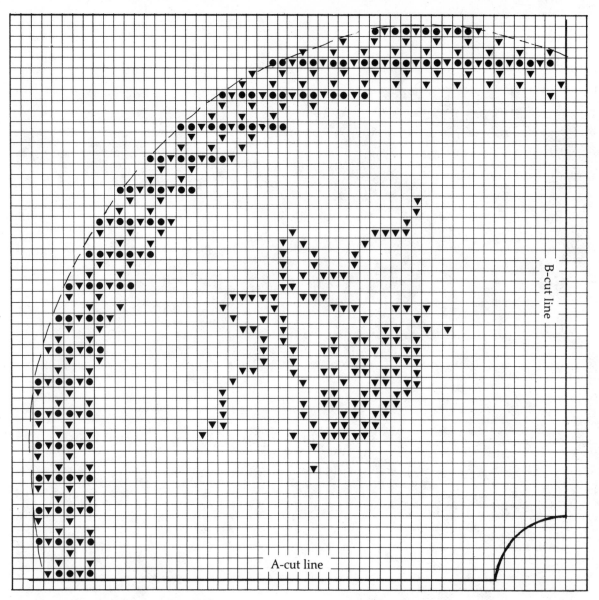

B-cut line

A-cut line

Form cone by overlapping A and B. Bind seam.

▼ violet

● white

Cornucopias made from paper were popular tree ornaments in the past. This needlepoint cornucopia is made to last, while giving your tree an old-fashioned flavor.

The technique is practical only if you are making several ornaments, as you begin by dying the canvas to give it an antique color.

Materials: #10-count mesh canvas (for each ornament you will need 8x8 inches); 1–2–3 Persian-type yarn in colors indicated on diagram; Rit dye (old rose, aqua, lavender, blue); needle.

Directions: Dye the canvas according to directions on the Rit dye package and let dry.

Use a Continental stitch and follow the diagram. Do not fill in the background. The effect of the needlepoint in contrast to the dyed canvas is what makes this ornament distinctive.

When complete, cut out the canvas in the shape shown on diagram. Overlap the edges a few meshes and bind them with a yarn matching the color of the dyed canvas. Attach a loop of yarn at the top of the bound edges for hanging.

Felt forum

Felt is the most popular material used to make Christmas ornaments because of its many advantages. It is soft in texture but is fairly sturdy to work with, which makes it easy to cut and stitch accurate shapes. No hems or seams are required. You can glue it to itself when adding decorative trims. It can be used for flat decorations as well as stuffed ornaments. Because of the wide assortment of colors, any design is possible. Further, most fabric shops, five-and-tens and craft stores sell 9x12-inch pieces of felt, which makes it economical to create a variety of colorful ornaments. Every scrap piece can be used for something.

The patterns that follow are all actual size. Most of them are basic shapes that can then be individualized with lace, ribbon, buttons, sequins, bells and other trims. This is a good time to get out those odds and ends of scraps. The tiniest piece of lace on Mama bear's blouse will create the perfect collar. Tiny buttons and other notions sold in hobby shops for dolls' clothes are just right for these projects. Once the basic pattern is made, the fun of dressing each cat or bear can lead to some pretty creative decorations. Let your imagination take over once you've made a few. Each member of the family can be represented. For example, give the Cool Cats personality. Put jeans on one for your teenager, clothe another in a sequined dress, add initials to Mama's apron. If you enjoy embroidery, add decorations in this way.

General information: Trace the patterns provided and cut out each piece. No seam allowance has been provided, as you will stitch as close

to the cutting line as possible. If you are using another fabric, allow ¼ inch for a seam.

In order to position the details on the face, for example, you can use the drawing of the finished project as a guide or transfer the details onto the felt. (See page 13.)

Pin the pattern to the felt and trace an outline around each piece. If you are making several of the same ornament, pin 3 or 4 layers of felt together before cutting out each pattern. Since felt has no grain, you can cut the pieces out any way to conserve the fabric.

Cut out all the little details with sharp scissors. A paper punch is a good tool for making perfect eyes, buttons, cheeks and a mouth.

Often it is easier to attach details before stitching the final project. If the pattern calls for double bonding of felt, use a small amount of white glue. Fusible webbing such as Stitch Witchery can be used to bond large pieces together. This will stiffen the material and will give substance to the body.

A light padding is used for all of these projects. In some cases you may want more fullness. The bear, for example, can be stuffed with polyester batting to give it roundness.

Each finished ornament has a hanging loop which is made from embroidery thread. Use 6 strands to make a 2½-inch-long loop of a matching or contrasting color to go with each ornament. Insert this between the front and back at the top or in an appropriate place before stitching around the edge.

Penguin

Materials: small piece of white felt, white thread, black thread, quilt batting, button or sequin for eye.

Directions: Trace the pattern of the penguin, including the center piece. Cut out and pin to 2 layers of felt and cut out. Either cut center piece from paper pattern or transfer onto white felt. Cut 1 piece. Cut 1 piece of polyester batting slightly smaller than the pattern.

If you want a fat or rounded penguin, you can stuff it with loose polyfill after it is stitched. However, these felt ornaments have been designed to go together, and each is only slightly padded to give them dimension.

Pin the white center to the front of one black piece and stitch around the edge with white thread. Place the batting between the front and back of the penguin and insert a loop of embroidery thread at the top of his head for hanging. Stitch around the outside edge with black thread.

Add a little pearl button or sequin bead for the eye. It can be sewed or glued in place.

Contented cat

Materials: 2 pieces black felt makes 3 ornaments, white pencil, black thread, 2 rhinestone sequins, 6 inches ⅛-inch pink satin ribbon, bell, embroidery thread, scrap of pink felt.

Directions: When working on black felt, you can use the pattern in one of the following ways. First, trace the pattern from the book on plain white paper. Cut out and pin to the felt so there is enough room left on the felt for 2 more cats. Draw around the outline with white pencil. Repeat 2 or more times. Punch through the tracing with the pencil to mark the tail and ear outline. Sandwich batting between felt squares and stitch. Cut each out as close to stitching as possible.

The second way is to pin the paper pattern to a double layer of felt and cut out 2 pieces for each ornament. Cut a separate piece of batting slightly smaller and stitch the felt pieces together with batting between.

If you want a fat cat, stitch the front and back of the cat together, leaving a small opening at the bottom. Stuff with loose polyfill and stitch across the opening.

Cut a small pink triangle and glue in position on the ear. Glue a rhinestone sequin or button in position for the eye. Hand-stitch the narrow ribbon around the neck and tie a bow. Attach a bell if desired.

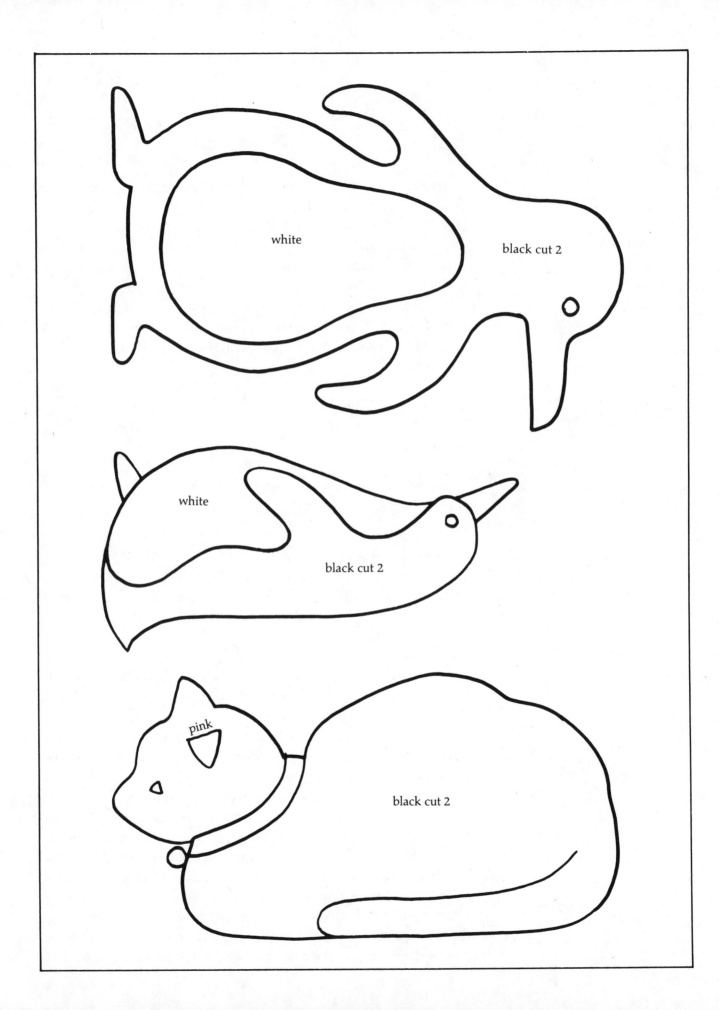

Papa bear

Materials: 2 pieces caramel-colored felt squares for 4 bears, scrap of red and black felt, black thread, paper punch, polyester batting, small piece of black embroidery floss.

Directions: Trace the bear pattern 4 times on 1 piece of caramel felt. Trace the coat pattern 4 times on red and the pants 4 times on black.

Sandwich batting between the two pieces of caramel felt with the outline of each bear on top. Stitch around each outline with black thread. Cut out each body as close to stitches as possible.

Cut out 2 layers of felt for each pair of pants and stitch the 2 pieces together at side edges. Turn right side out and slip onto the bottom of each bear.

Cut out each red coat and put on each bear. Use the paper punch to make a black button and glue each in position on the coats.

Embroider each face with 2 strands of black floss and add a hanging loop at the top of each head.

Mama bear

Materials: 2 pieces of caramel-colored felt squares for 4 bears; 2 pieces blue felt; scraps of white, pink and red felt; scrap of lace; black embroidery floss; black thread; glue; batting.

Directions: Trace the bear pattern 4 times on 1 piece of caramel felt. Trace the body of the dress 4 times on blue felt. Trace apron pattern 4 times on white and cut out small pieces for pockets, collars, buttons and bottom trim of dress.

Place felt with outlines of each bear on top of 1 layer of batting and another piece of caramel felt. Stitch around the outline and cut each out close to stitches. Place blue felt pattern on another layer of felt and cut out 2 for each bear. No batting between layers.

With 1 dress piece on the front and back of each bear, stitch around edges. Glue apron and details to front of dress. Add lace trim over arms on either side of dress. Use 2 strands of black floss to embroider details on each face. Add hanging loop.

mustard cut 2

Teddy pops

Materials: 2 pieces mustard-color felt squares; scraps of pink, black and red felt; glue; black thread; small piece red and black embroidery thread; paper punch; 4 lollipops.

Directions: Trace 4 teddy patterns (see p. 13) on one piece of felt. Pin this to a second piece of felt with batting between. Stitch around the outline of each pattern and where arms, legs and head join body. Stitch face or hand-embroider.

Cut out each ornament. Use the paper punch to make red felt buttons and pink inside-ear parts. Cut a black piece for the nose. Clip edge of pink circles to fit. (See finished drawing.) Glue buttons, ears and nose in position. Tie a piece of red embroidery thread around the neck and tack a loop to the top for hanging.

Fold end of one arm around a lollipop stick and tack it to itself. Hang several of these teddy pops on your tree for all the children who come to visit.

Papa bear

Mama bear

bodies-caramel

vest-red

white

pants-black

dress-blue

Circus cat

Materials: 2 pieces of brown felt for 6 ornaments; 2 pieces blue felt; scraps of red, green, pink, black and yellow felt; black thread; black embroidery floss; batting, glue; paper punch.

Directions: Trace 6 heads, 12 hands on brown felt. Sandwich batting between felt pieces and stitch around outline of each pattern piece. Cut out each piece. Cut 12 feet pieces from black felt.

Trace body onto blue felt 6 times. Sandwich batting between layers of felt, and stitch center lines and down outside edges only. Leave neck, end of arms and bottom open. Cut out each shape.

Slip neck into top, hands-and-feet pieces between body, and stitch openings. Cut 2 hat pieces for each ornament and stitch together. Glue to top of head. Glue little flower shapes in different colors to the front and back of clown's suit. Use a paper punch to make circles and glue to the center of each flower (available precut in package from variety stores).

Embroider face details with 2 strands of black embroidery thread in a backstitch. Add hanging loop.

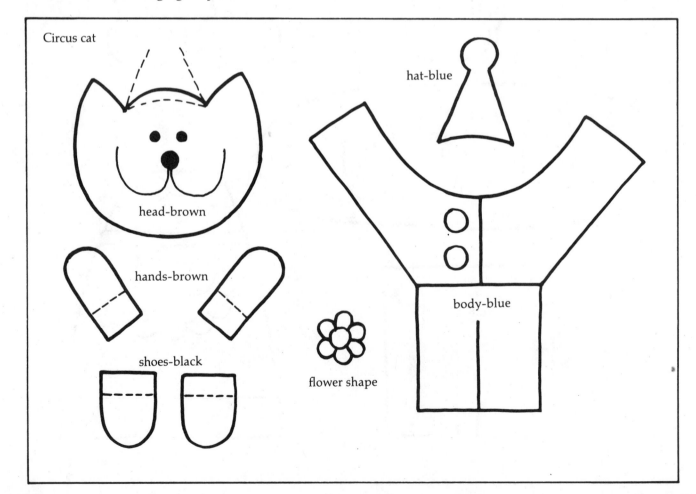

Circus cat

head-brown

hands-brown

shoes-black

flower shape

hat-blue

body-blue

Angel cat

Materials: caramel, white, pale pink and bright pink felt pieces; polyester batting; black and white thread; 6 inches of pink embroidery floss; small piece of black floss; 3 inches of eyelet.

Directions: Trace the pattern for each piece onto felt. The colors for each piece are indicated on the pattern. With batting sandwiched between 2 pieces of felt, stitch around head and arm pieces. Cut out as close to stitches as possible. Black stitches accentuate the outline of these parts.

With batting between 2 pieces of white felt, stitch along side edges below wings and across the bottom. Cut this out. Sandwich batting between wing pieces and stitch around outline. Cut out.

Insert arm and wing pieces on either side of body and insert neck of head into the top. Stitch all open edges.

Cut one piece of bright pink scalloped edge and place a piece of eyelet even with top edge. Stitch this to the underside of the bottom edge of body.

Finish the angel cat with an embroidered face made of 3 strands of black embroidery floss in a backstitch and French knots for eyes. Tie a pink embroidery thread bow around the neck and attach a hanging loop at top corner of body.

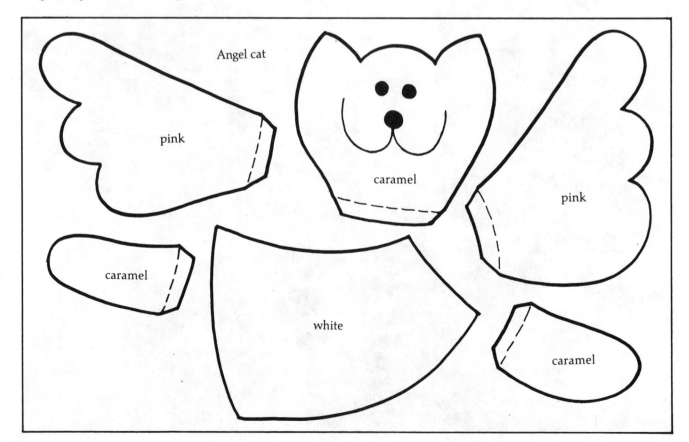

Angel cat

pink

caramel

pink

caramel

white

caramel

Cool cats

Materials: 2 light brown felt squares for 4 ornaments, 2 pieces red felt squares, scrap of white felt, black and red thread, black embroidery floss, batting, glue.

Directions: Trace 4 cat patterns on brown felt and 4 coats on red felt. Sandwich batting between the 2 brown pieces and stitch around each cat with black thread. Cut out close to stitches.

Cut a double thickness for each coat (not batting). Place the one-piece coat on front, with another piece on the back of each cat, and stitch around edges with red thread.

Fill in eye and nose area with black thread and stitch with 1 strand in a backstitch along the mouth lines.

Cat in the hat: Cut and stitch cat pattern as above. Cut double layer of red coats and hats. Cut strips of white felt for coats and hats.

Place coat and hat pieces on the front and back of each cat and stitch around the outer edges with red thread. The hat can be glued to the head. Glue strips onto front and back of red felt. Add a hanging loop to the top of each and stitch face details as above.

Cool cats

body-light brown

coat-red

stitches

stitches

coat and hat-red and white

Folk doll

This is a basic pattern for a felt doll ornament that you can dress up any way you want. It can be a little girl with yarn hair and a smocked pinafore. It can be dressed in jean pants and checked shirt, or you can adorn it with a basic felt dress to which you will add lace, rickrack and other trims.

Farm boy

Materials: 1 square caramel felt; scrap piece of black felt; small piece of print fabric and denim; batting; 1/8 inch yellow ribbon; dark brown yarn; red and black embroidery floss; feather trim; glue.

Directions: Trace and cut out doll pattern as with peasant girl. Trace shirt pattern on printed fabric and cut out 2 pieces. Trace and cut out 2 pieces for overalls from denim. Trace and cut 2 pieces for hat and 1 piece for each shoe from black felt.

Stitch front and back of shirt and overall pieces and put them on doll's body. Attach yellow ribbon straps at either top corner of overalls. Cross straps in back and tack to overalls.

Make hair from dark brown yarn and tack to head. Stitch 2 pieces of hat together, place on head and add tiny feather trim. Glue black shoes on each foot.

Use 3 strands of embroidery floss and fill in eyes with black and mouth with red. Attach a piece of yarn in back of his head for hanging.

Peasant girl

Materials: 1 square pale pink felt; scrap pieces of black, white and red felt; white cotton eyelet; yellow yarn; batting; red and black embroidery floss; glue.

Directions: Trace doll pattern on pink felt. Place batting between this and another piece of pink felt, and stitch around outline. Cut out.

Trace shirt pattern on white felt and.cut 2. Trace and cut 2 pieces for the skirt, 1 piece for the bib and 2 strips 3 inches long.

Stitch front and back of shirt and skirt pieces at side edges, and put them on the doll's body. Attach straps to either top corner of the bib and stitch lower edge of bib to top edge of skirt. Cross straps in back and tack to skirt.

Trim each shirt sleeve with a piece of eyelet and do the same around the waist. Glue small pocket pieces to the front of the skirt. Glue black shoes on each foot and tie embroidery floss around each ankle.

Cut 6 strands of yellow yarn 10 inches long. Find the center and tack to the top of doll's head. Tack at each side and braid the strands on either side. Tie ends with yarn or satin ribbons.

Use 3 strands of embroidery floss and fill in eyes with black and mouth with red. Attach a piece of yarn at the back of her head for hanging.

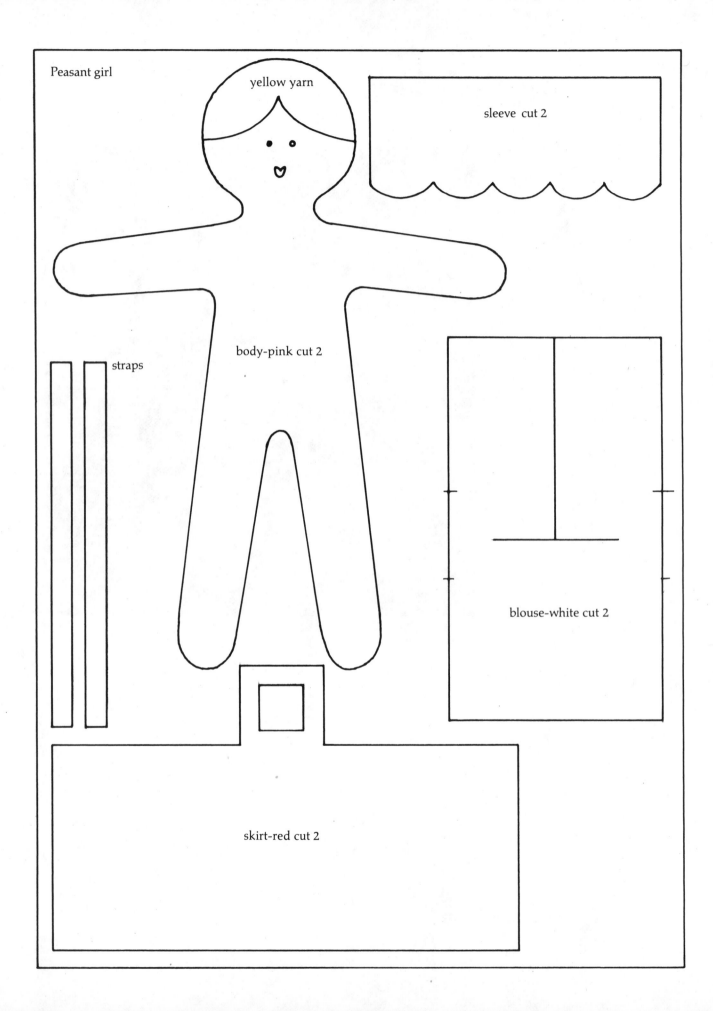

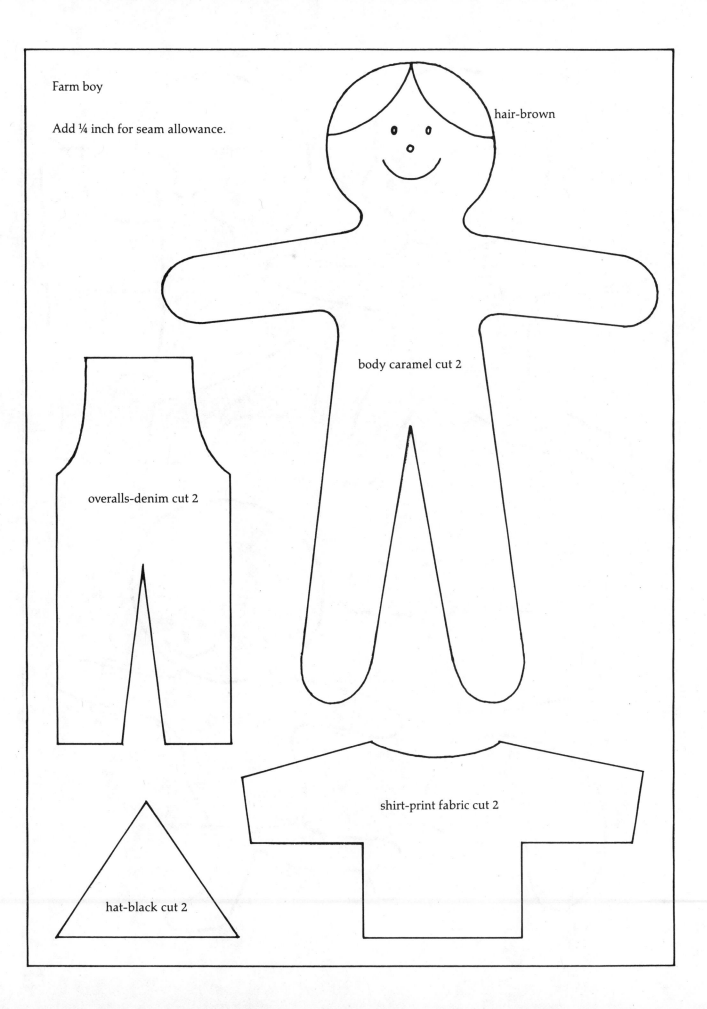

Farm boy

Add ¼ inch for seam allowance.

hair-brown

body caramel cut 2

overalls-denim cut 2

shirt-print fabric cut 2

hat-black cut 2

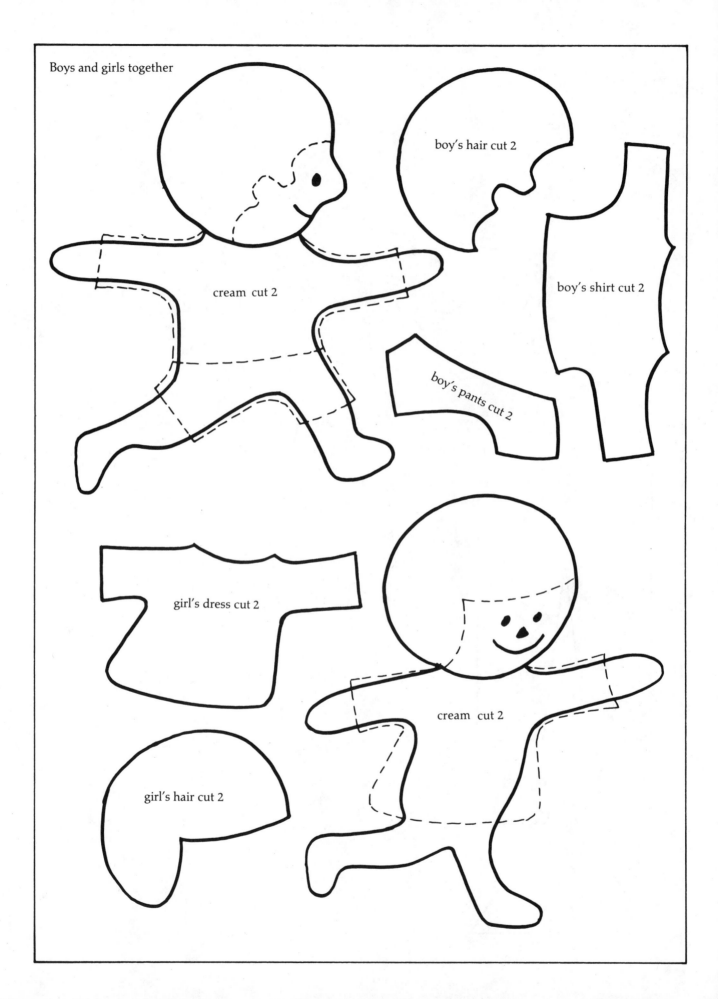

Boys and girls together

boy's hair cut 2

boy's shirt cut 2

cream cut 2

boy's pants cut 2

girl's dress cut 2

cream cut 2

girl's hair cut 2

Boys and girls together

These little ornaments are attached at the hands with tiny pieces of Velcro. If you make enough they can be strung around the tree, and after Christmas the children will love playing with them. This is an ideal crib or carriage toy as well.

Materials: 2 cream-colored felt pieces will yield 4 ornaments; 2 pieces blue felt; scraps of red, bright pink, orange and brown felt; white thread; black embroidery floss; paper punch; polyester batting; package of Velcro; 4 inches lace trim.

Directions: Trace 2 boys and 2 girls on 1 piece of cream-colored felt. Trace 2 hair pieces for each ornament. Trace shirts and pants and dresses.

Sandwich batting between 2 cream felt squares and stitch around each outline. Cut out as close to stitches as possible. Cut double layers for all other pieces.

Place front and back of each hair piece on the 4 ornaments and stitch around the outside edge. Stitch front and back of clothing and slip onto the bodies. Tuck into boys' pants and stitch across the waist through all layers. Add lace to girls' dress hems, and glue pockets, collars, buttons and other details to clothing. Use 2 strands of black floss and make French knots for each eye.

Tack a small dot of Velcro to each hand. Remember to plan carefully so that corresponding pieces of Velcro match the hands that will grasp one another.

Not a creature was stirring

This stocking is made entirely of felt pieces. The appliqué illustration is made up of basic, easy-to-cut shapes, and the embroidered words can be machine- or hand-stitched.

Materials: 2 red felt pieces 12x16 inches; 9x12-inch squares of white, black, blue and gray felt, black embroidery floss; white glue; paper punch.

Directions: Enlarge stocking pattern and transfer to one large piece of red felt. (See page 13.) Cut 2 stocking pieces. All the rest of the pattern pieces are shown same size. Trace and transfer each pattern piece to the color felt indicated. Cut 8 mice. Use a paper punch to cut out 16 white circles for eyes. Cut 16 small black pieces for eyeballs and 8 black triangular shapes for noses.

Glue each piece to the front of one stocking piece in the following way. First, place the headboard of the bed in position. Next, glue the pillow down, followed by the sheet and then the blanket.

Next, glue a row of 4 mice so their noses overlap the edge of the blanket. Glue the remaining 4 on the pillow with noses over the edge of the sheet. Glue eyes and noses in position on each face and embroider whiskers with 3 strands of black floss.

Transfer the saying to one piece of the cuff. Cut 2 pieces. Embroider the saying by machine or hand with 3 strands of black floss in a backstitch. Pin the embroidered cuff to the front of stocking and stitch across the top edge. Repeat on the back of stocking.

With wrong sides together, stitch around outer edge of stocking. Add a ribbon loop inside the top edge for hanging.

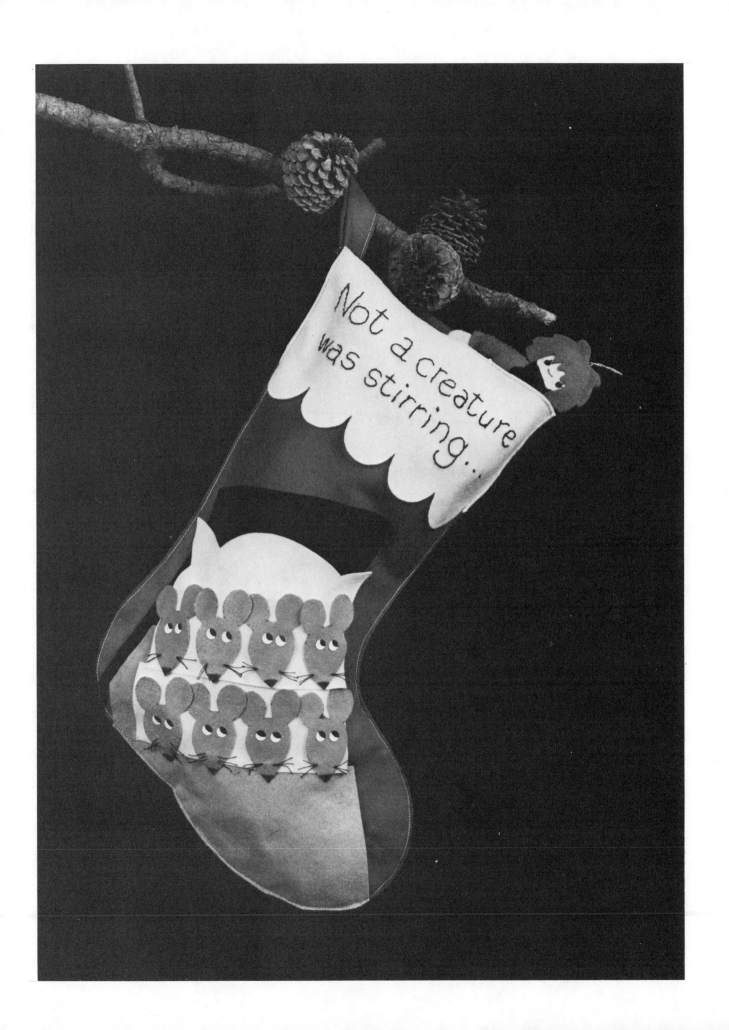

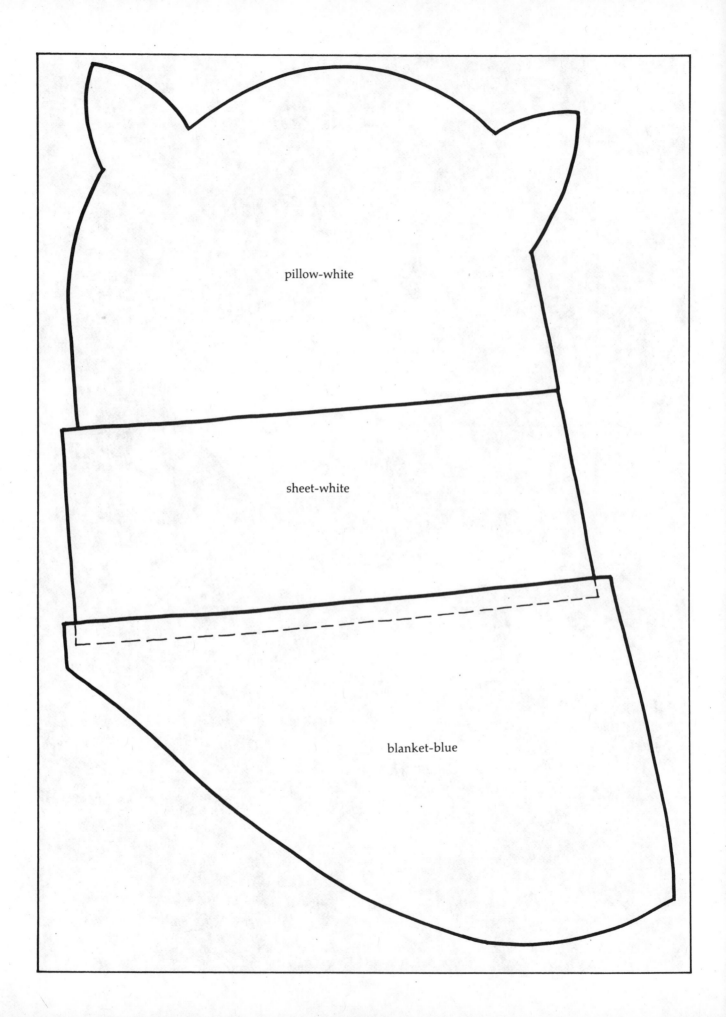

pillow-white

sheet-white

blanket-blue

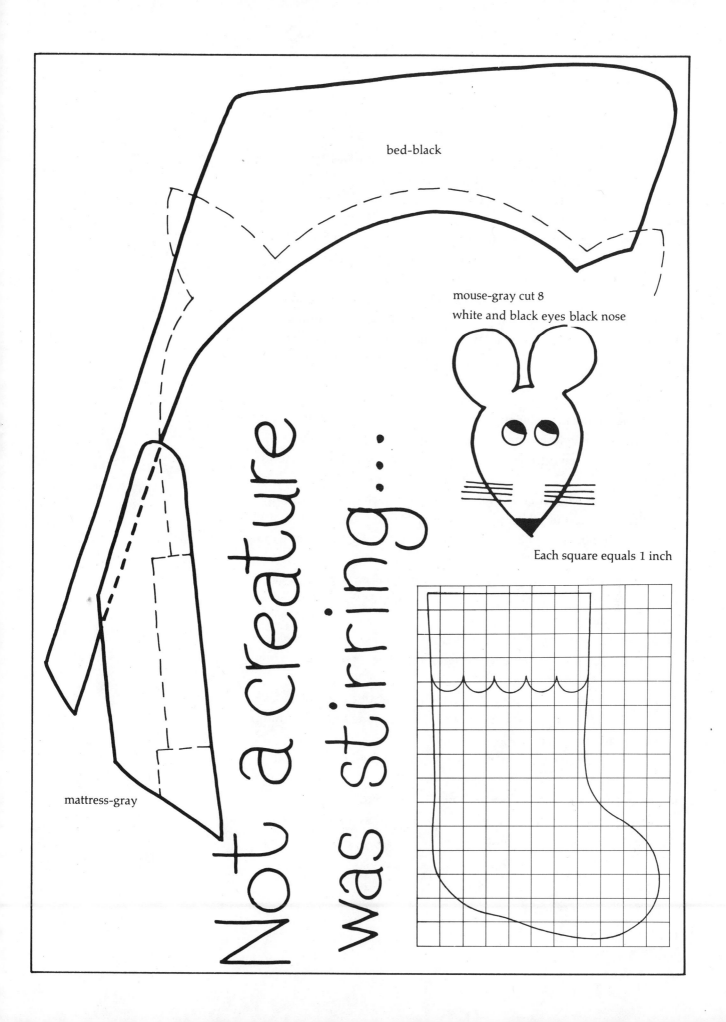

bed-black

mouse-gray cut 8
white and black eyes black nose

Each square equals 1 inch

mattress-gray

Not a creature was stirring...

Elf stocking

This project reminds me of a jester's stocking and I was tempted to design it with a pointed toe. Christmas protocol dictated a more conventional approach, and my daughter Lisa thinks it looks like an elf's stocking.

At Christmastime most five and ten cent stores carry red and green felt pieces 12x18-inches in addition to the usual 9x12-inch pieces that come in all colors. This stocking can be made from 2 green and 1 red felt piece. It is not padded. If you'd like to do this, however, add quilt batting to the list of materials and cut 2 pieces of fabric for lining.

Materials: 1 piece of 12x18-inch red felt, 2 pieces 12x18-inch green felt, 6 large bells, white embroidery floss, 6 inches ½-inch red ribbon, graph paper, white chalk.

Directions: The stocking is 15 inches long. Each square on the grid equals 1 inch. Transfer the pattern to graph paper. (See page 13.) Tape the tracing to a window pane with the green felt piece over this. You should be able to see the outline in order to retrace with the chalk onto the felt.

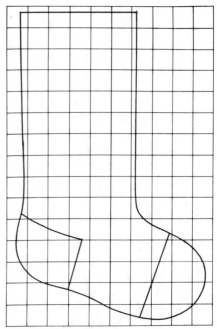

Each square equals 1 inch

Trace the cuff pattern and the heel and toe which are shown same size. When cutting out all pieces add a ¼ inch seam allowance. Cut 2 green stocking bodies. Cut 2 pieces for the cuff, 2 heels and 2 toes from red felt.

Pin the heel and toe in position on the front and back pieces of the stocking as indicated on the pattern. Stitch along the straight edge only of the heel and toe pieces.

With wrong sides together pin the front and back of the stocking together and stitch along the edges leaving top edge open. Trim seams as close to the stitching as possible.

Transfer the letters from page 116 to the front of one cuff piece. Use 2 strands of white cotton floss and embroider the name with a running or back stitch. (See page 44.)

Place right sides of the cuff pieces together and stitch side seams. Turn right side out and place the cuff over the top of the stocking matching top edges. Stitch around ¼ inch from the top.

Fold ribbon in half and tack inside top edge of stocking. Attach a large bell to the end of each point of the cuff.

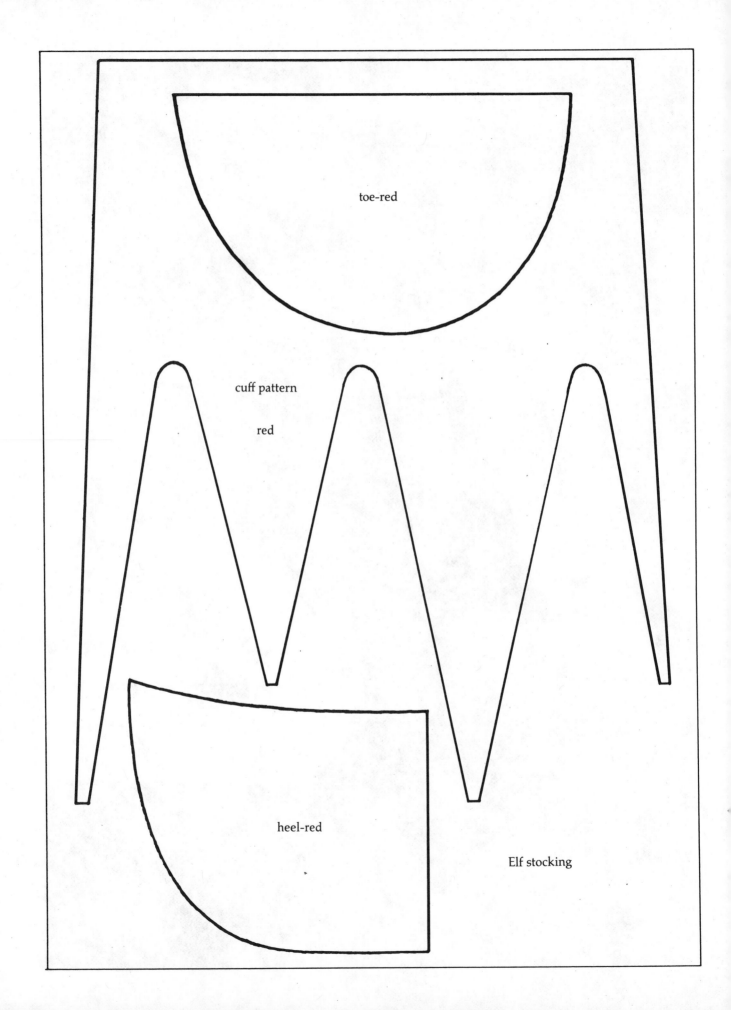

toe-red

cuff pattern

red

heel-red

Elf stocking

Paper and wood

The variety of designs found in paper products such as wrapping paper, wallpaper, Con-Tact paper and shelf paper gives us endless possibilities for decorative, colorful ornaments.

Paper is as easy to craft with as fabric, often easier. Consider paper patchwork. There is no seaming, piecing and stitching involved, but the visual effect is that of a multicolored project.

When making paper ornaments, the first thing to do is collect some interesting papers. As with fabric, scraps of paper can also be recycled. Discontinued wallpaper sample books can be obtained for the asking from your local paint and wallcovering store. This will give you more than enough color, texture and design to make all the combinations you want. Save wrapping paper from gifts and, if wrinkled, iron them flat before using. Magazines provide another source, and, when the pages are cut up imaginatively, can yield some exciting ornaments for totally cost-free decorations.

Most of us use the same equipment for all our craft projects. However, when working with paper there are certain tools that will make it easier and help to create more professional results. It has taken me many years to adjust to using my sewing scissors for fabric and another pair just for cutting paper, which tends to dull them. It has been even harder to resist using scissors at all in favor of a razor or craft knife, which always guarantees a sharper, straighter, cleaner cut. A metal ruler is another invaluable tool against which you can hold the blade for accuracy in cutting.

A T-square and triangle will enable you to make perfect angles, and rubber cement is often a cleaner, neater and easier adhesive to use than glue for some paper projects.

Posterboard in assorted colors; large rolls of tracing paper for making same-size patterns; graph paper in many sizes; and Fom-Cor, a ¼-inch lightweight foam material sandwiched between shiny white paper, and other materials familiar to designers and artists can be used by the craftworker.

Paper patchwork stars

While patchwork is usually a sewing technique, it is used here in a simplified version that I have adapted many times for various projects in my books. At one time I covered a blanket chest with paper patchwork, and for *The Great Bazaar* I covered a craft box. Each time the results looked like fabric patches but were much easier to achieve.

This is a perfect technique for Christmas ornaments because you can make as many variations as you can find paper patterns. Best of all, they cost nothing. If you don't use paper scraps left over from wallpaper or wrapping paper, you can purchase enough paper to make dozens of ornaments for very little cost.

They take practically no time to make, and in one evening your family can create enough to fill the entire tree. This is an especially good way to make extra ornaments at the last minute.

Materials: a variety of papers such as wallpaper, wrapping paper or Con-Tact, posterboard, razor blade or scissors, glue or rubber cement.

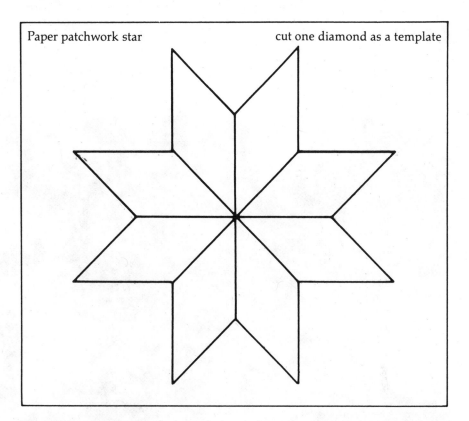

Paper patchwork star — cut one diamond as a template

Directions: Trace the diamond shape from the diagram provided and transfer to a piece of cardboard. Cut this out and throw away the diamond piece. You will use the cutout hole as a guide.

When planning your ornaments, consider making each section a different pattern, or use 2 papers cut 4 times each. You might combine light and dark colors, or patterns and plains, or red and green or silver and gold, for examples.

Make 2 stacks of 4 papers each and place the cutout of the diamond shape on the top. Trace the outline on each stack of papers. Use a razor blade and straight edge to cut through the layers of paper. You will have 8 perfect diamond shapes.

Apply white glue to the back of each piece of paper and arrange them so they butt together on the posterboard. (See diagram.) When you have formed a star, cut this out. Tape a piece of string to the back for hanging.

Making in quantity: It is as easy to make these in quantity as to make one. Decide how many you will need. Select the papers and place them face down on your work area. Coat the backs of all papers with rubber cement and leave to dry. This will take a minute or so. Coat the poster-board with rubber cement and let this dry.

Stack the papers on top of one another. They will not stick as long as 2 coated sides don't touch. Use your cutout diamond shape to trace the outline on the top of the paper and cut out as before.

Arrange the pieces on the coated posterboard to create as many stars as needed. They will stick together. If you make an error and must remove one piece, use rubber-cement thinner to do so.

Country charmers

The basic quality of these ornaments is their simple charm. All the designs are silhouettes of familiar shapes cut out of posterboard covered with paper or fabric, or they are made of balsa wood which is cut out and stained or dyed. The flat quality is part of their appeal.

Some of the designs are American folk figures reminiscent of early American weather vanes, such as the running horse and angel. Along with the traditional designs, we've mixed some barnyard and woodland animals and Christmas shapes, which are treated in the same way. For example, if you want to have a traditional early American country-style tree, you would select the more traditional shapes to cut from balsa wood. When dyed with regular fabric dyes, such as Rit, in faded pastel colors of old rose, pale aqua, Shaker blue and heather gray, they have a country charm similar to the antique handmade ornaments and decorations found in homes 200 years ago.

Country prints by designers like Laura Ashley and Pierre Deux help us to create this same charm in another way. The delicate French coun-

try style works just as well on these shapes, and it is easy to cover both
sides with scraps of fabric.

Wallpapers and wrapping paper in small overall country patterns
provide us with yet another area of crafting, and it is often easier to
cover the shapes in this way while achieving the same effect.

While the shapes alone are quite nice, it is the selection of the papers
or fabric that will make your tree exquisite. Even though you will need
only a small amount of material for each, take the time to select colors
and patterns that design well together.

The directions are the same for cutting patterns from posterboard or

balsa wood. Balsa wood is often easier to cut; however, a sheet is 3x36 inches, and some of the ornaments are too large to fit the 3-inch-wide area. Therefore you will use posterboard for these projects. Both materials are available in the five-and-ten.

General directions for all ornaments: You will need the following materials for all ornament shapes: 1 sheet of 3/32-inch balsa wood or a sheet of posterboard, a selection of fabrics and papers, white glue or rubber cement, rubber-cement thinner, X-Acto craft knife with a #11 blade, sharp needle, nylon thread, pencil, tracing paper, cutting board or thick cardboard.

p. 108

p. 93

p. 86

p. 42

p. 162

p. 18

p. 38

p. 168

p. 46

p. 49

p. 55

p. 52

p. 126

p. 114

pp. 129, 141, 138

p. 35

p. 32

p. 165

p. 144

p. 132

p. 32

p. 70

p. 72

p. 75

p. 30

pp. 64, 66

p. 81

p. 68

Covering with fabric: Cover the entire piece of posterboard or balsa with a thin coat of glue. Place the fabric onto the glued surface and smooth down so no wrinkles or air bubbles appear. A metal ruler is good for this purpose. Repeat on the back with the same fabric or a contrasting fabric.

Covering with paper: Coat the surface of balsa or posterboard with a thin coat of rubber cement and set aside to dry. Coat the back of the wrapping paper or wallcovering with rubber cement and let dry. Carefully place the coated paper on the coated balsa or posterboard and smooth down. If there are wrinkles or air bubbles, remove paper with the rubber-cement thinner and reposition. Do not attempt to pull it off without the thinner as it will rip. No added rubber cement is needed when repositioning.

Trace the desired shape and transfer (see page 13) to the fabric- or paper-covered posterboard or balsa wood. Place this on a cutting board or thick cardboard surface. Carefully cut around the outline with a sharp X-Acto knife.

Thread a sharp needle with 12 inches of nylon thread and find the point at which your ornament will balance when hung. To do this put a threaded needle into a point on the top of the ornament and let the ornament hang from the thread. When the accurate spot is located, pierce the ornament with threaded needle as close to the top as possible and tie a 6-inch nylon loop for hanging.

Dyed balsa ornaments: This crafting technique is practical only when making several ornaments, but it's a cinch to make 50 at once.

Trace and transfer the shapes as many times as possible on a sheet of balsa wood. Cut each out with an X-Acto knife as described above.

Dissolve the Rit dye in hot water as directed on the package. You will need a separate pot of dye for each color used.

Use a needle to thread a loop of nylon thread through the top of each ornament. Use this to hold each piece while dipping into the dye. In this way you can dye both sides at once and hang each up to dry. The longer you hold each piece in the dye bath, the darker the color you will get. In this way you can create various ornaments in different shades of the same color.

Stained balsa ornament: You will need Minwax wood stain, a 2-inch sponge brush, a clean cloth, Krylon clear spray varnish.

Using an inexpensive sponge-type brush, coat each side of a sheet of balsa wood with stain. Honey or Walnut produces rich tones. Follow the directions on the can for best results. When dry, give each side a coat of spray varnish and let this dry.

Trace and transfer each ornament shape as described above and hang from a loop of nylon thread.

Create a romantic touch when hanging these on each tree branch. Make fat bows of lace-covered muslin and tie each where an ornament is hung. The combination of the simple flat country shapes and the lace-textured muslin is quite nice.

Swingers

Materials: balsa wood, colored felt-tip markers, 24 inches of black embroidery floss, glue, needle, X-Acto knife.

Directions: Trace and transfer the boy and girl figures to balsa wood. Cut each out with an X-Acto knife. Cut the little piece for each swing ½ x ½ inch.

Color each area of the figures according to the patterns. Poke holes through each hand where indicated. Glue the bottom of each ornament to the center of each swing piece. Let dry thoroughly before picking it up.

Use 1 strand of embroidery thread for the swing ropes. Run thread down through one hand and through one end of the swing. Continue under and up the other side. Create a loop for hanging and tie 3 inches from the top.

Variation: If you prefer, you can make the hair, clothes and face on each ornament from felt rather than coloring them on.

Trace each piece, transfer to felt squares, cut out and glue into place.

Trees for the tree

These little paper hang-ups can be made in a variety of patterns. The country style comes from combining 2 different small-print papers in the Christmas tree design. Each becomes a three-dimensional ornament.

Materials: gift-wrapping paper in small prints, stiff paper such as a file folder, rubber cement or white glue, ballpoint pen, metal ruler or straight edge, razor, tracing paper, pencil, string or embroidery floss for hanging.

Directions: Coat the back of a piece of wrapping paper the size of a file folder with glue or rubber cement. (If using rubber cement, let dry and coat folder. Let dry.) Place the wrapping paper on the folder and smooth down. Cut this down to 7x8 inches. Turn face down.

Transfer the pattern of the rectangle and the triangle top to the back of the file folder. Each side of the finished ornament will be 2⅛ inches

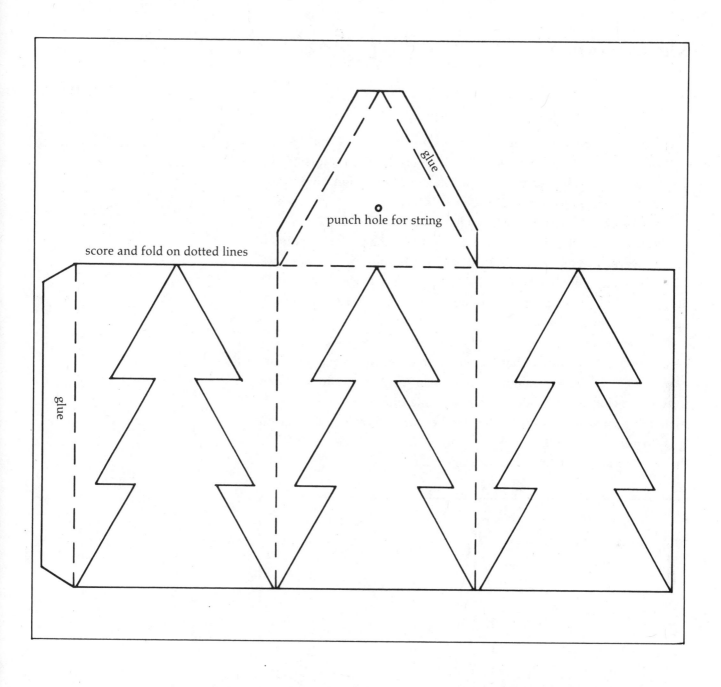

score and fold on dotted lines

punch hole for string

glue

glue

wide and is marked by a dotted line on the pattern. In addition, there is a ¼-inch flap for gluing. Score all dotted lines by running a ballpoint pen against a straight edge down each line on back of file folder.

Next, transfer 3 tree shapes onto a different patterned paper. Cut out and glue into position as per diagram. Each tree will fit between the scored edges.

Cut around outline of pattern with straight edge and razor. Fold the scored edges against the straight edge until they crease smoothly. Cut an 8-inch piece of string and fold in half. Thread through top (triangle) at center dot and knot on the underside.

Fold gluing flaps on top and side, and glue ornament together with white glue. Use an elastic band to hold it while drying. Hang from string loop on top.

Mexican ornaments

These star-shaped ornaments are made from ordinary spring-type clothespins. The folk quality comes from the bright paint colors of red, green, orange, purple and yellow. This color combination gives these ornaments their festive south-of-the-border feeling.

Two versions of the star are shown here. Diagram #1 is the easier to do because the clothespin heads fit together to form a perfect 5-pointed star. However, if you can't find this exact clothespin in your area. we have provided another star that involves an extra crafting step. (See diagram #2.) Look at the shape of the clothespin for each so you can find the appropriate ones.

Either version is easy to make and costs very little, especially considering the fact that you will have wooden ornaments that will last forever. If you want to leave them in their natural state or stain and then varnish the clothespins, you can create a whole different theme.

Materials: package of spring-type clothespins, a variety of Krylon spray-paint colors, Elmer's Glue-All, strip of balsa wood, craft knife (balsa wood and craft knife for diagram #2 only).

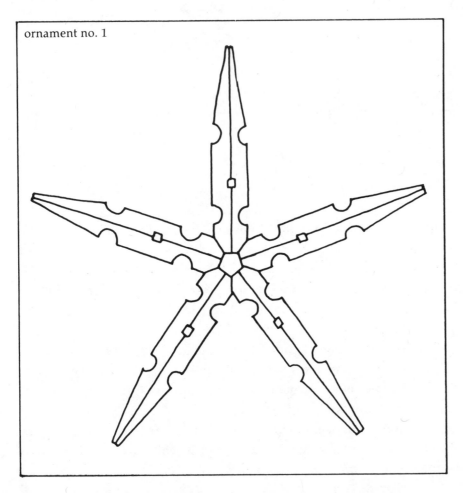

ornament no. 1

Directions: Remove springs from the clothespins so you have 2 wooden pieces. You will need 5 clothespins for each ornament. Spray-paint each set a different color. Let dry.

Place the 2 pieces of each clothespin back to back and glue together to create 5 points of the star. If you are using clothespins such as those found in diagram #1, place a piece of waxed paper over the diagram to use as a guide, then attach the head of each star point together with a dab of glue. Leave this to dry before attaching a hanging loop.

To create the star ornament in diagram #2 you will glue each painted piece back to back as above. Then paint the strip of balsa wood and cut 2 circles for the center front and back of the ornament.

Place a piece of waxed paper over the diagram and center 1 wood circle, unpainted side up. Spread glue over the surface of the disk and place the head of each star point so they meet in the center of the disk. Spread glue on the unpainted side of the other disk and place this on

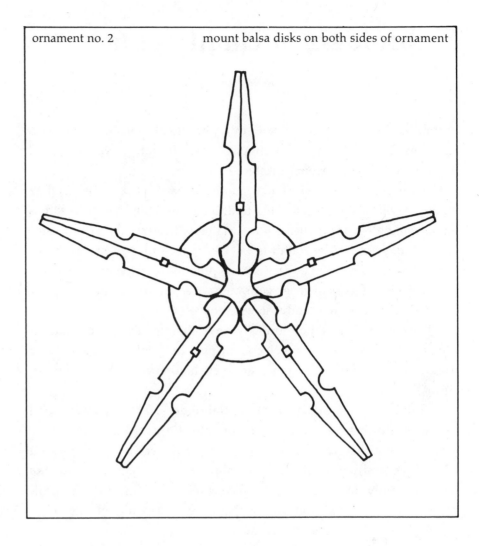

top. Leave to dry before attaching a loop of embroidery thread to the back of one point.

Making in quantity: This project is impractical and costly if not made in quantity. However, if you cover your tree with these ornaments, it will be a colorful as well as a practical way to decorate for the holidays.

Take all the clothespins apart and divide them into 5 equal parts. Spread newspaper in a well-ventilated area, preferably outdoors, and spray each group with a different color paint. When dry, they must be turned over and repainted.

If you are making the star from diagram 2, paint a long strip of balsa wood. Make a template of the disk from cardboard and use this to mark the number of circles to be cut out.

Trace the diagram several times on a large sheet of paper, place the wax paper over this and glue your pieces together, lining them up with the diagram which you can see through the paper.

Embroidery enchantments

Embroidery is a wonderful way to create illustrations on Christmas stockings. The work can be as simple or as elaborate as you like, and the results will be pure enchantment.

The various stitches (see stitch guide on page 44) can be used to outline or fill in the design. This traditional method of needlecraft is one of the oldest and is usually associated with early American samplers. Today embroidery affords us the opportunity to create beautifully decorated Christmas accessories quite inexpensively. If you had to buy them, the cost to cover your entire tree would be quite high.

Embroidery has many advantages, one of which is its portability. You'll be surprised at how quickly an elaborate illustration can be completed in spare moments. You can pick up your embroidery and work for 15 minutes here and there, and before you know it you've created an heirloom.

Almost any fabric can be used for embroidery. The ornaments and stockings shown here are done on cotton, satin or even-weave linen. You may find that you'd like to make a very special velvet stocking which is generally more difficult to embroider, as is delicate fabric like silk or organdy. In my last book, *Making It Personal,* most of the projects were embroidered, and the few that were made with delicate materials had to be worked very carefully.

Transferring designs for embroidery

The embroidery designs are presented full-size so no scaling is necessary. This is particularly important when looking for your own designs to transfer. There is no question that the design possibilities are greatly expanded if you feel confident enlarging any pattern you want to use. However, it is much easier and more accurate if you have a same-size drawing to work from.

How does the design get from the book onto your material? There are different methods that produce better effects on some material than others. For example, satin is a lovely fabric for making stockings. Many of the transfer pens sold commercially for transferring designs tend to bleed on this material. Some methods work better than others on dark colors. If light passes through your material when it's held up to a window, the easiest and most accurate way to transfer a design is the following: Use masking tape and secure the traced design to the windowpane. Position the fabric over the drawing and tape at all 4 corners so the material is taut on the pane. Use a soft pencil and retrace the design onto the fabric.

The next-best way to transfer a design is to trace it from the book, then retrace it on the back of the tracing paper. Place this over the fabric and burnish over the outline with a blunt object, such as a butter knife.

If you need a darker image, the best transfer pencil or crayon is one that is washable. This can be transferred from the tracing paper onto your fabric, and the dark blue lines will enable you to see the lines where your stitches will go. When finished, if any lines show, you can easily remove them with a damp cloth.

A transfer pencil or crayon is another product that is used to transfer a design with the use of a hot iron. You draw the design with the pencil, then place it face down on your material and press it with a medium-hot iron. It's a good idea to do a test first to be sure the pen markings don't bleed on the fabric. All transfer products are sold in most notions and art needlework stores.

Materials and tools for embroidery

No matter how small a project you will do in embroidery, you should not be without a good embroidery hoop. This keeps the area you are working on taut so the stitches won't pull and pucker your fabric.

The vast array of colors found in embroidery floss is enough to send anyone's imagination soaring. Every five-and-ten as well as notions and art needlework stores sell a good selection of cotton floss. I've found that DMC is a good brand, and their line includes gold and silver threads as well as pearl cottons.

A thimble, selection of needles, and small sharp scissors complete your essentials for doing embroidery, so you can see why it continues to be such a popular way to handcraft. The combination of design potential for painting with thread, the few tools needed, the fact that you can work in small increments of time and the relative inexpensiveness makes it most attractive. Finally, the finished project is one of lasting beauty.

Twinkle, twinkle, little star stocking

Polished cotton is delicate in appearance, yet sturdy enough for a stocking. The embroidery can be as detailed or as simple as you want. This old-fashioned nursery illustration is outlined with 1 color on the machine, with the details done by hand in a backstitch. You can fill in the entire scene with a variety of colors if desired.

The full size alphabet is for personalizing a name on the cuff.

Materials: ¼ yard pink polished cotton, small piece of white piqué for cuff, black thread, black embroidery floss, embroidery hoop, sharp needle, quilt batting.

Directions: Transfer the pattern and illustration to the fabric. (See page 112.) Place the area to be hand embroidered in a hoop and outline with 3 strands of floss. Any areas to be filled in with a solid color, such as the hair, can be worked with a satin stitch. (See stitch guide page 44.) To avoid tangling of thread, pull strands apart, then put back together and thread needle. The wallpaper in the background is done with a chain stitch. The center of each design on the cover is a French knot, and all others are back- or running stitches.

Trace the letters for the name and retrace on the back of the paper so the transfer will read correctly. Place the tracing on a piece of white piqué large enough to fit in an embroidery hoop. Transfer tracing onto the fabric by rubbing over the back of each letter. Embroider with 2 strands of black floss.

Cut out 4 pieces of fabric for the body of the stocking. The pattern includes a ¼-inch seam allowance. Cut 2 pieces of batting slightly smaller. Sandwich batting between back 2 pieces and front 2 pieces, with embroidery design to the outside. Baste each group together.

Machine-stitch around the quilt, bed, bed skirt and around pillow and window frame to quilt the illustration if desired.

With right sides facing, stitch front and back of stocking together at side edges. Leave top edge open. Clip around curved areas on seam allowance. Turn right side out. Pad your ironing board and steam-press from the back of the stocking with embroidery side face down.

With right sides facing, stitch short ends of 2 cuffs together. Repeat with other 2 pieces. Place one cuff over the embroidered cuff and stitch around the bottom edge. Turn and press. Place the cuff inside the top of the stocking with the wrong side out and pin top edges together. Turn a 6-inch-long ½-inch-wide ribbon in half lengthwise. Insert the ends under the cuff so it's lined up with the corner edge. Stitch around the top edge, catching the ribbon loop between all layers.

Turn the cuff over the edge to the front of the stocking so it covers the top edge of the embroidered design on the stocking.

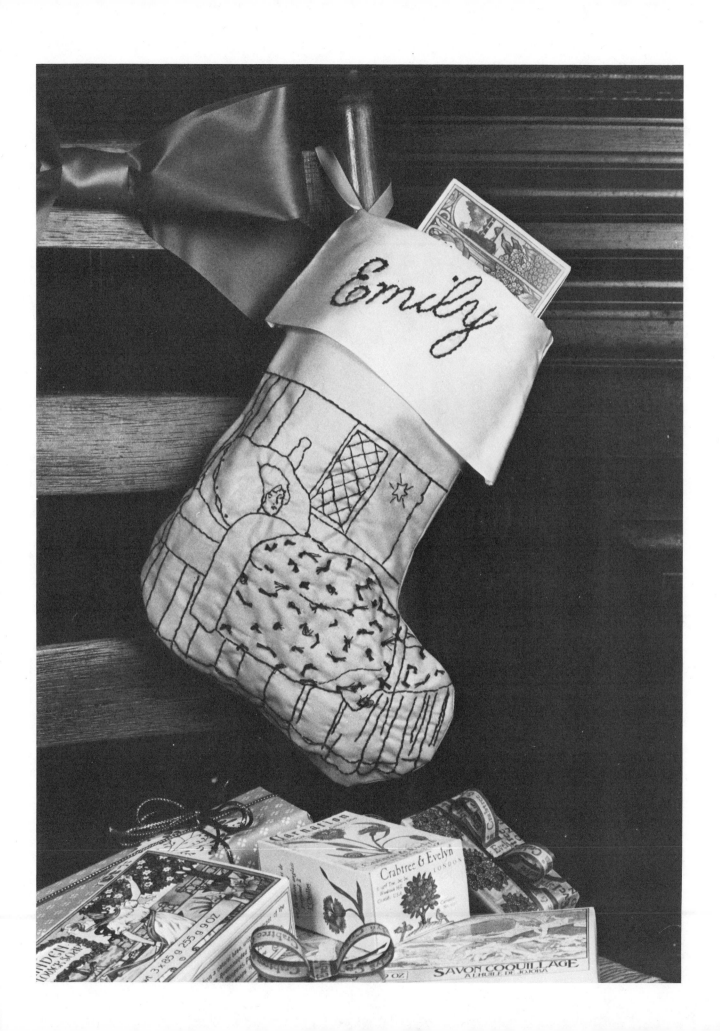

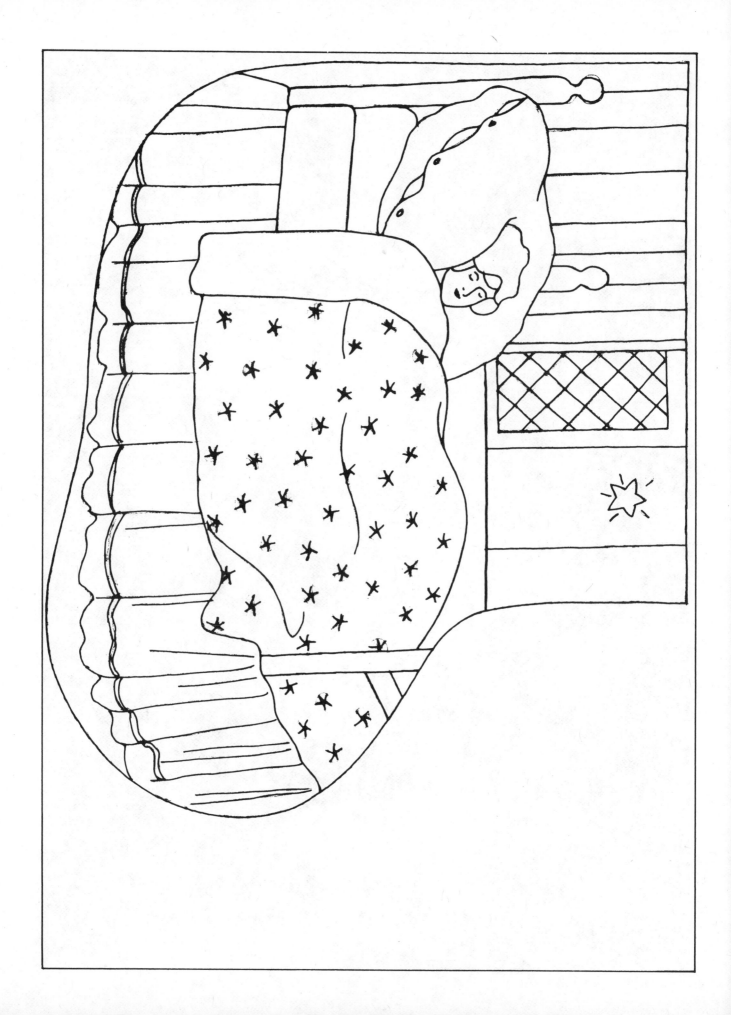

Star light, star bright stocking

This is another old-fashioned nursery illustration that evokes a feeling of holiday charm. The illustration is given same size and will fit on this small-size stocking. However, if you want to enlarge the stocking, you can still transfer the illustration as is to a larger pattern.

Materials: ¼ yard blue polished cotton, dark blue embroidery floss, batting, white satin or taffeta for cuff, 6 inches ½-inch blue ribbon, embroidery hoop, needle.

Directions: Trace the stocking pattern and illustration onto polished cotton. (See page 112.) Do not cut out. Put fabric in embroidery hoop. Use 2 strands of floss to outline the star, hair, face, hands, window and shirt in a backstitch. The wallpaper pattern is a lazy daisy stitch and a French knot. (See stitch guide page 44.)

Cut 4 pieces for stocking, adding ¼ inch all around for seam allowance. Cut 2 pieces of batting slightly smaller. Sandwich each batting piece between 2 layers of polished cotton and baste.

Machine-quilt front stocking piece by stitching the outline of bed, pillow, bed covers, window frame and sill if desired.

With right sides together, stitch around edges with top open. Clip around curves in seam allowance and turn right side out. Press from the back.

Trace the letters on paper and retrace on the back. Transfer to a piece of satin large enough to fit into embroidery hoop. Backstitch with 2 strands of embroidery floss. Cut 2 pieces of folded fabric so you have 4 layers for the cuff. With right sides together, stitch side seams.

Place the cuff wrong side out to the inside of the stocking. Be sure that seams match up and the embroidered name is toward the front. Stitch around the top raw edge. Turn cuff out over the stocking.

Pet stockings

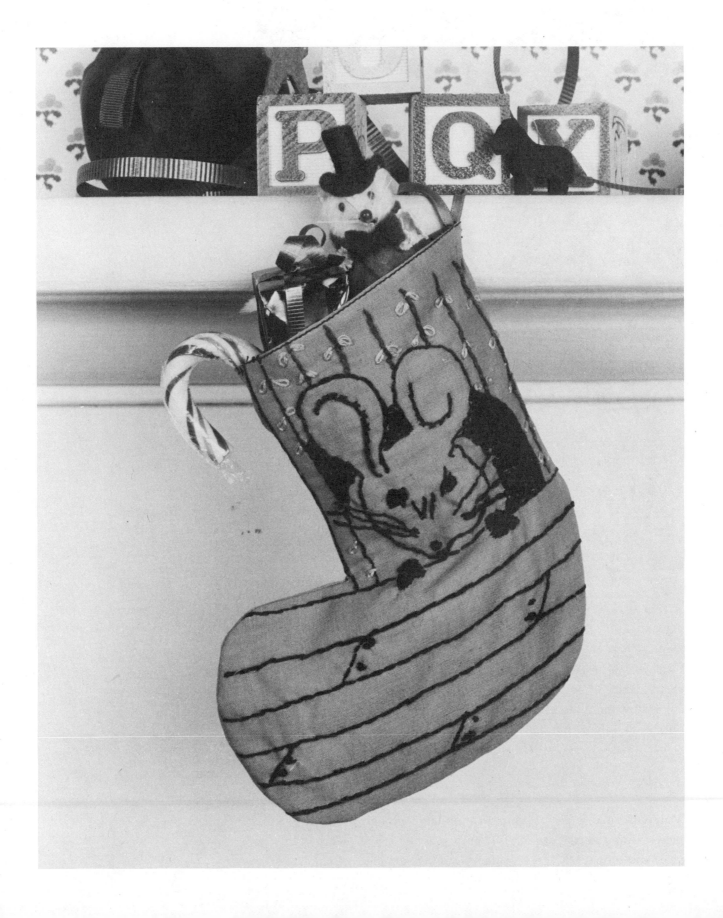

Don't leave out the family pet when hanging stockings and ornaments. These mini-stockings are just the right size for kitty's new toy. Or if you want to make them for tree ornaments, insert a small gift or candy canes in each one to hang on the tree. If you use scraps of colorful material, each will look different. The embroidery is a simple outline, and the appliquéd kitten is made from one round piece of felt.

Kitty

Materials: small piece of printed cotton large enough to cut 2 stocking pieces same size as pattern, 9x12-inch piece of white or gray felt, red pearl and brown DMC embroidery floss, white paper, pencil.

Directions: The pattern is shown same size. Trace and transfer to back of fabric. (See page 124.) Add ¼ inch for seam allowance and cut 2 pieces. Trace the cat. Turn the paper over and retrace. Place this tracing on the felt and rub over the outline with the end of a pen. Cut this piece out and pin to the front of one stocking piece.

Transfer "kitty" to a piece of white felt with enough material around the area to be embroidered so it will fit in an embroidery hoop.

Use 2 strands of red floss and use a backstitch. Cut out a 2x3/4-inch rectangle with the name centered within.

Turn the top edges of each stocking piece under ¼ inch, press and turn another ¼ inch. Slip-stitch. Stitch top edge of cuff to top edge of front stocking piece. Use 2 strands of brown embroidery floss to outline details on sleeping cat.

Pin stocking pieces together with right sides facing. Stitch around edges and clip curves in seam allowance. Turn and press. Tack a ribbon loop to one side seam for hanging.

Not even a mouse

Not just for kitty, this wee stocking is adorable for baby's first Christmas. Just scraps of material, a few embroidered stitches and a few minutes of your time are all that's needed.

Materials: piece of tan polished cotton large enough to cut 2 stocking pieces same size as pattern; brown, blue and black embroidery floss; hoop; sharp needle.

Directions: Trace and transfer the pattern and design to a piece of tan polished cotton. Do not cut out. Place the fabric in an embroidery hoop. Use 3 strands of brown floss to create floorboards with a backstitch. The knots in the floor are made with a French knot.

Create striped wallpaper with a chain stitch of blue floss. Outline the mouse and whiskers with a backstitch of brown floss. Fill in the eyes and nose with black embroidery floss in a satin stitch. (See stitch guide page 44.) Now fill in the hole area with small cross-stitches in black.

With fabric doubled, cut out 2 stocking pieces ¼ inch larger all around and leave an extra ½ inch at the top edge.

Turn top edges under ¼ inch and press. Turn another ¼ inch to wrong sides of each piece and press. With right sides together, pin the front and back pieces at the sides and bottom. Stitch together, leaving the top edge open. Blind-stitch the top edges. Clip all around on seam allowance and turn right side out. Press and add a hanging ribbon loop to the inside at one corner seam.

Counted cross-stitch perfection

Anyone can do cross-stitch and every piece will be perfect. These two qualities have kept the counted cross-stitch high on the list of popular needlecrafts for as long as women—and now men too—have held a needle and thread.

Long before I began using this technique, Jon had mastered the craft as I sat in awe watching him create a sampler with apparent ease. I didn't realize then what I now know: that the beauty of its guaranteed perfection is its greatest attraction. Every stitch is exactly like the others, and the finished project is neat and crisp. You don't need a printed design on fabric to follow as with embroidery, or a painted design on canvas as with needlepoint. The design is charted on graph paper, and each square represents one cross or X stitch of the fabric. As you fill in the stitches on the material (according to the chart), the picture emerges. You can create a saying or personalize a project with a name or initial in the same way.

You can do cross-stitch in one color or with many colors for a realistic illustration. This needlework is done with a blunt embroidery needle and embroidery floss. Depending on the weight of the fabric, you will use all 6 strands or fewer down to a single strand for a fine weave.

Any even-weave fabric, such as Hardanger or Aida cloth (available in needlework stores), can be successfully used if you count the threads for placement of the stitches. Any graph or checked fabric, such as gingham, can be used for this crafting technique, and the size of the checks will determine how large your design will be. For example, one stitch will fill each check, so it's easy to see that a large pattern is not the most desirable.

For the best results, stitch all lines slanted in the same direction and then the other. All top threads should cross over in the same direction.

Cross-stitch stars

A star motif is the most popular in early American designs. Typically it was used in crafting techniques, such as stenciling, patchwork, appliqué and cross-stitch. This is a simple but classic design for quick crafting on grid-patterned fabric to match the Scandinavian snowflake stocking on page 141. The stars are done on green, while the stocking is done on a red background. This is another example of a good portable craft.

Materials: grid-patterned fabric (see source list), white embroidery floss, needle, embroidery hoop, polyfill.

Directions: Trace the star pattern and transfer to the fabric, leaving enough fabric around the star to fit in an embroidery hoop. (See page 113.)

Follow the charted diagram for placement of stitches. Use all 6 strands and draw the thread up from under the fabric. Do not make a knot. Leave 2 or 3 inches hanging. You will then catch this under several stitches to secure as the work progresses. Work all stitches in the same direction. Then cross all stitches going in the opposite direction. If you must stop during your work time, remove the fabric from the hoop to avoid permanent creases.

When finished, pull the last 2 or 3 inches of floss under several stitches on the underside of the work. Again, do not make a knot. Remove from the hoop and press on the wrong side of the fabric.

Make a double thickness of material and cut 2 stars. With right sides together, stitch around, leaving 1 side of 1 point open for stuffing. Turn right side out and fill with polyfill until the star is quite puffy. Stitch opening and attach a loop of ribbon or embroidery floss for hanging.

Making in quantity: When making several, trace the star pattern and transfer to a piece of cardboard. Cut this out and use as a template to draw several stars on the fabric. If you arrange them one after the other, you can do all the cross-stitching at one time and then cut out each star. As you go from one project to the next, you will be creating a whole cloth filled with cross-stitch stars which gives one a feeling of real accomplishment. You may decide to pad the whole thing and make a wall hanging of one large piece with lacy stars. The cross-stitch design looks like snowflakes.

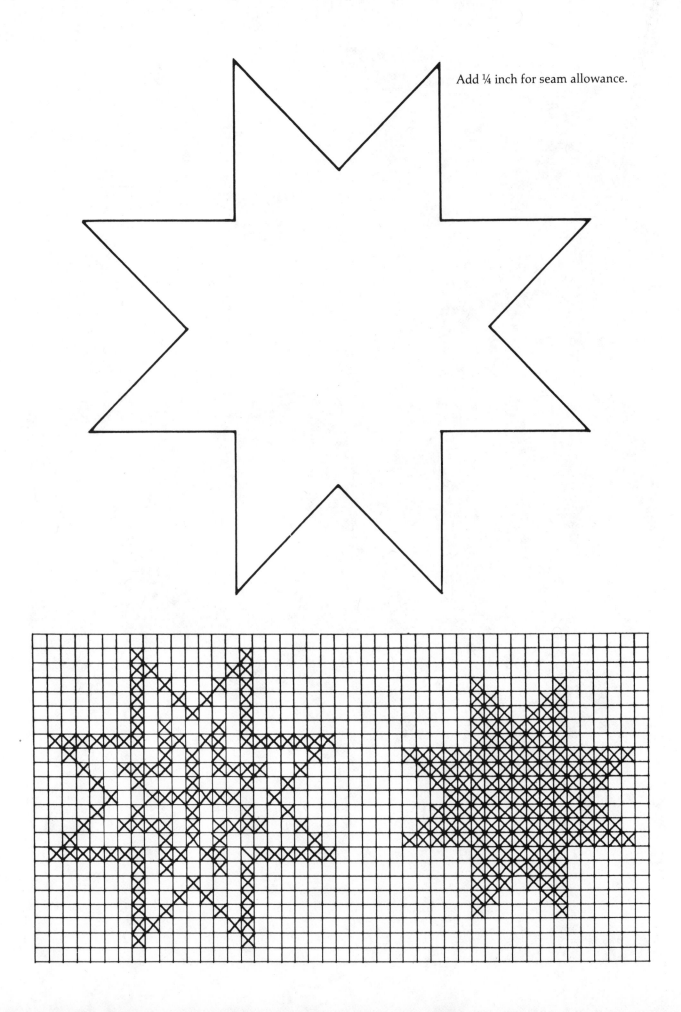

Add ¼ inch for seam allowance.

Baby's first stocking

The toy soldiers standing guard on this stocking cuff are done in cross-stitch on Aida cloth. This is the perfect gift or project for your own baby's first Christmas. You can spell out the child's name if it fits the cuff area or do as we have here.

This is a simple project that has a crisp neat look that can be achieved only with the cross-stitch. When you've made one stocking, you'll surely want to make others for any of baby's older sisters or brothers.

The pattern is shown full-size so no enlarging is necessary.

Materials: small piece #14 Aida cloth large enough to fit in embroidery hoop (art needlework shops); pale pink, pastel green, rose, blue and black embroidery floss; embroidery needle; hoop; ¼ yard pastel printed cotton fabric; polyester batting; ¼ yard lining fabric.

Directions: Follow the chart for placement of stitches on the cuff. Use 3 strands of embroidery floss in colors indicated. Begin by separating the 3 strands, then put them back together and thread the needle. This will keep the floss from becoming tangled.

Insert the cloth into the embroidery hoop. Do not knot your thread. Start at the center square, bring your needle up from the underside and leave 2 inches hanging. (See page 125 for cross-stitch directions.)

Trace the stocking pattern on plain white paper and cut out. Pin to a double layer of printed fabric. Use the pattern to cut out 2 stockings from lining as well. Cut 2 slightly smaller pieces of batting.

Pin together 1 lining piece, 1 piece of batting and 1 piece of printed fabric right side up. Repeat with the other 3 pieces for the back.

On each lining, mark off diagonal lines spaced 1 inch apart. Do this in the other direction. (See diagram.)

Quilt through all 3 layers of each piece by stitching along these lines. With right sides together, pin back to front, leaving top edge open. Stitch along edges. Trim seams and clip in every inch or so at each curved area. Turn right side out.

Cuff: Center the finished embroidery within an area 2½x5 inches on the Aida cloth. Allow an extra ¼ inch all around for seams and cut 2. Cut 2 pieces same size from the lining fabric. With right sides facing, sew short ends of cuff together.

Sew short ends of lining together. With right sides together, place lining cuff over Aida cuff. Stitch along bottom edge. Turn right side out and press. Place cuff inside stocking with Aida side against lining of stocking. Match top edges and side seams. Insert a loop of ribbon on straight side of stocking and stitch along top edge. Trim seam and turn cuff to outside.

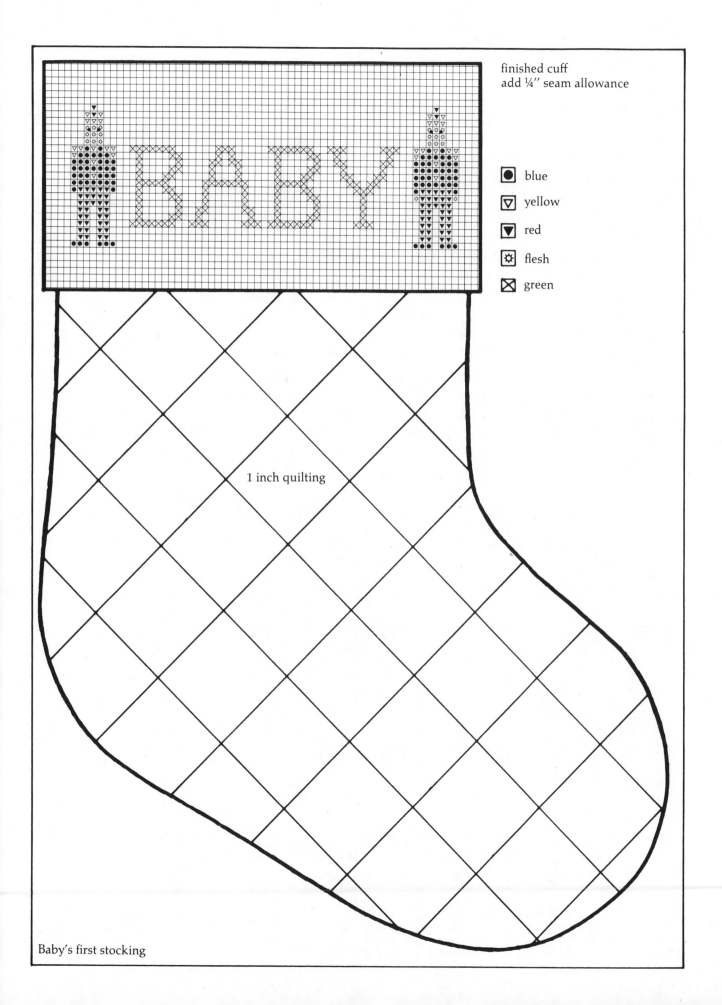

finished cuff
add ¼″ seam allowance

● blue

▽ yellow

▼ red

✿ flesh

⊠ green

1 inch quilting

Baby's first stocking

Personalized sachet ornaments

These little sachet pillows are made with Aida cloth, a little lace and cross-stitch. Personalize one for everyone on your list. Make them in white with bright red or green names, or use red and green Aida cloth and do your cross-stitch borders and names in white. After Christmas they make wonderful, sweet-smelling sachets for your lingerie.

Materials: Aida cloth 11 count (small ornaments are 4x4 inch, large are 4½x7 before hemming), red and green pearl cotton floss, embroidery hoop, red and green felt for backing, loose polyester fiberfill, lace trim, 8 inches ¼-inch satin ribbon for each ornament.

Directions: Do not cut Aida before doing the embroidery. Mark a pencil square for each ornament and insert fabric in embroidery hoop.

Follow the stitch diagram and cross-stitch each border and name. Cut out each finished piece ¼ inch larger. Baste lace trim at edge of pencil outline on each square. Cut felt backing same size as ornament and pin together with embroidered side between. Stitch all around, leaving 1 side open for stuffing. Turn, press and stuff. Add a drop of your favorite perfume to the stuffing and stitch opening. Attach ribbon at top corners and hang. If desired, add a little bow to top center.

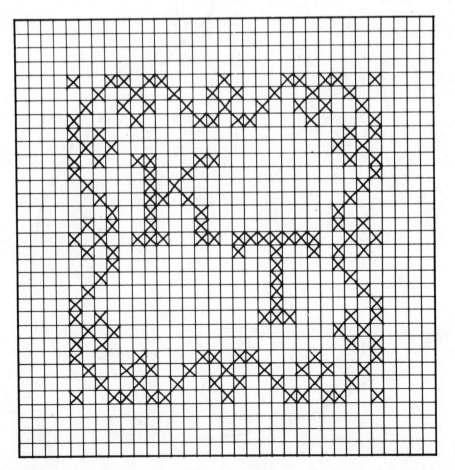

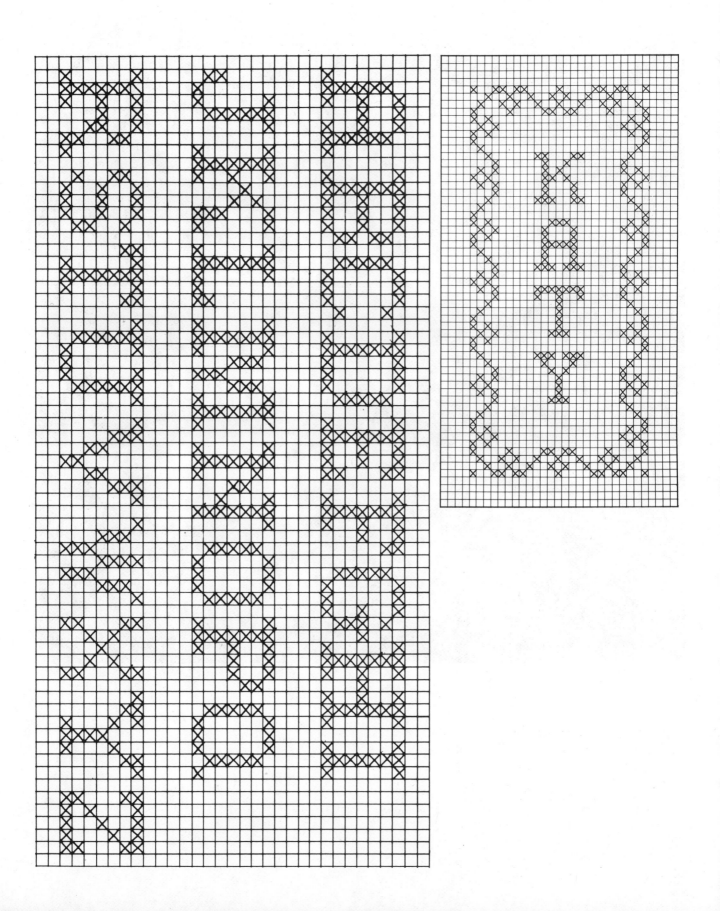

Stocking for a little angel

A cross-stitch border creates a crisp outline for a child's name. This personalized stocking is bound to become a favorite with your child year after year. The design is appealing for a young child's stocking and sophisticated enough for a teenager to appreciate.

The pattern can be used same size for a small stocking to hang by the fireplace or fill with small goodies and hang on the tree. If you want to make a larger stocking from this pattern, enlarge the design. (See directions on page 13.)

Aida cloth, commonly found in white, is also available in red and green. This makes it quick and easy to stitch a design in cross-stitch.

Materials: small piece of white #11 Aida cloth large enough to fit in an embroidery hoop, 12 inch long #14 red Aida cloth, 9x12-inch red felt piece, red, green, yellow, pale blue, pink, rose and white embroidery floss, 14 inches ⅛-inch green satin ribbon, 14 inches of eyelet.

Directions: Trace the pattern on bond paper and cut out with an extra ¼ inch for seam allowance.

Place red Aida in embroidery hoop and follow the charted design for cross-stitch angel. Pin the paper pattern to the Aida so the design is correctly positioned and cut out one piece. Cut a matching piece from the red felt for the backing.

Put the white Aida in the embroidery hoop and follow the charted alphabet on page 134 to cross-stitch the name and border with 3 strands of red floss. Cut a rectangle for the cuff 4x5½ inches. Turn edges under ¼ inch and press. Pin eyelet trim to the back of cuff on sides and bottom edge with satin ribbon on top edge. Stitch together.

Turn top edge of red Aida stocking ¼ inch to the right side and press. Pin red felt to front of the stocking and stitch together at the edges. Leave top edge open. Clip around curves in seam allowance and turn to right side. Press from back side.

Pin the top edge of the cuff to the top edge of the front of the stocking and slip-stitch together. Add a little green ribbon loop at one corner for hanging.

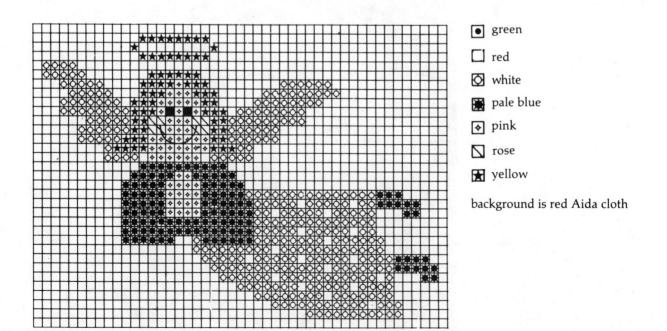

- ⊙ green
- ☐ red
- ◎ white
- ▨ pale blue
- ✦ pink
- ◩ rose
- ✴ yellow

background is red Aida cloth

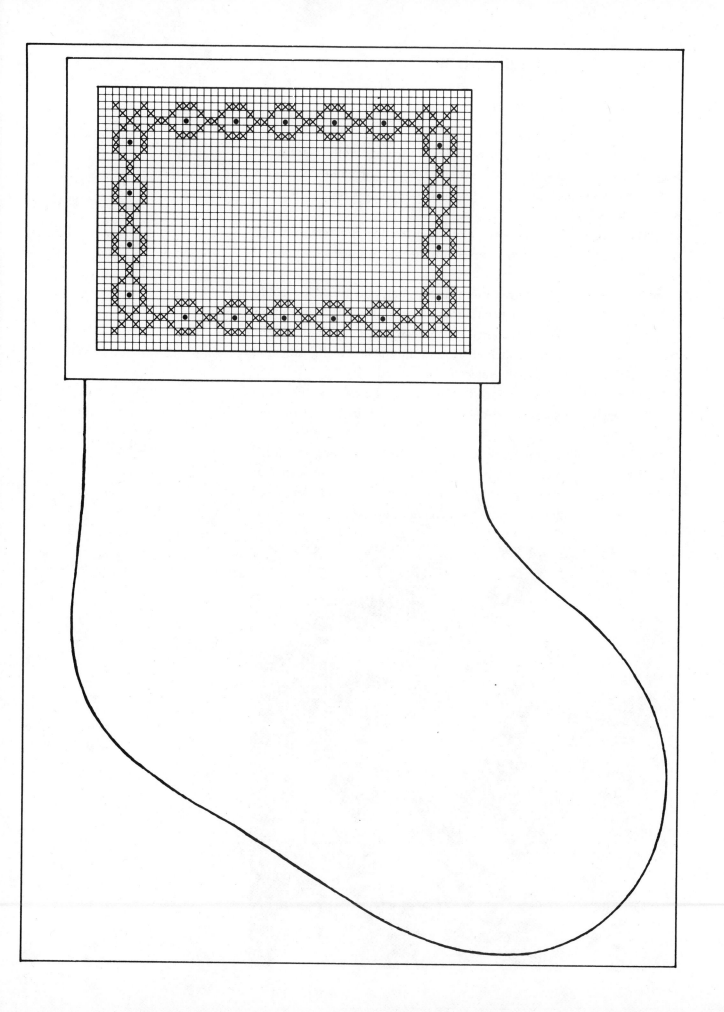

Prancing reindeer stocking

Bright red reindeer prance across crisp white Aida cloth. Add to the design brilliant green geometric trees and a border of white crosses on a red background and you have a repeat cross-stitch pattern worthy of any Christmas stocking.

Materials: 12x18-inch #14 Aida cloth, 12x18-inch red felt, red and green embroidery floss, embroidery hoop, needle, 6 inches ½-inch red satin ribbon.

Directions: Enlarge stocking pattern and transfer to the Aida cloth. Follow the chart for placement of stitches, beginning at the top corner with a band of red. When the cross-stitch designs are finished, cut the pattern out with an extra ½ inch all around the outside of the stocking shape. Use this to cut the same piece from the red felt.

Turn the top edge down ¼ inch to the back of the cross-stitch. Turn another ¼ inch, press and blind-stitch. The red band begins at the very top edge now.

Place the red felt on top of the cross-stitch stocking piece and stitch around outer edge with a ½-inch seam allowance. Trim seams as closely as possible and clip around curves. Turn right side out. Fold ribbon in half and attach at seam for hanging loop.

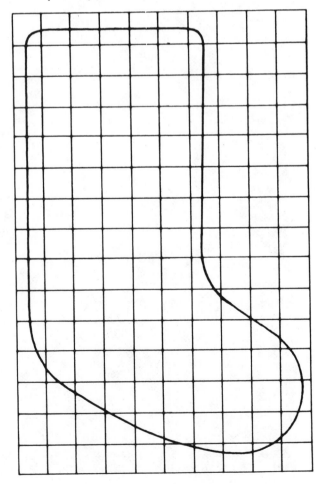

Each square equals 1 inch.

Scandinavian snowflake stocking

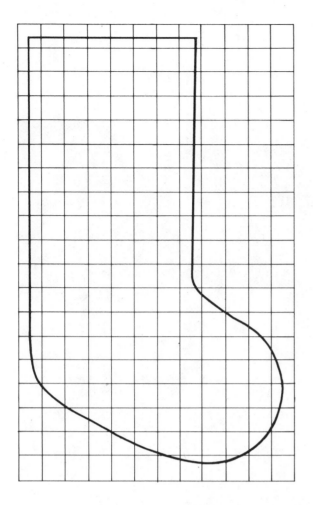

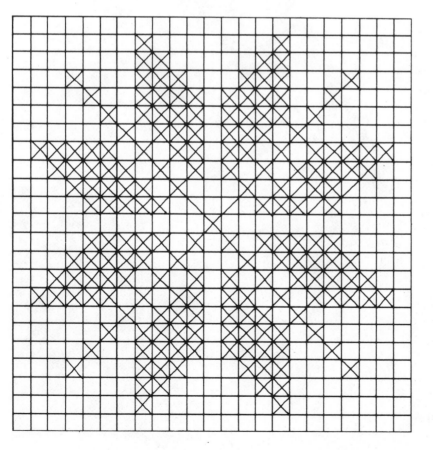

This snowflake pattern is used on the stuffed cross-stitch star ornaments as well (see page 126) and is easy to do in cross-stitch on a grid-patterned fabric. (See source list.) Each geometric star is identical, and if you make one or more, they will look quite handsome hanging in a row by the fireplace. The grid fabric comes in bright green, red, yellow, lavender and black. This stocking is red with crisp white snowflakes.

Materials: ¼ yard grid fabric, 1 piece red felt 12x18 inches, red thread, white embroidery floss, 6 inches ribbon, embroidery hoop, needle.

Directions: Enlarge the stocking pattern (see page 13) and transfer to the grid fabric. Do not cut out. Place the fabric in an embroidery hoop and follow the charted design. Each square of the fabric represents one cross-stitch. Because the squares are fairly large this project can be done quite quickly, and it's fun to see the design appear.

Cut out the stocking ¼ inch larger all around. Press from the wrong side. Use this to cut felt stocking piece. Press ¼ inch under at the top edge of the grid piece then turn another ¼ inch under. Slip-stitch this edge to 1 felt stocking piece.

Place piece of felt on top and stitch together, leaving open at top. Trim seams and clip around curves. Turn right side out. Fold ribbon to make loop and attach at corner for hanging.

Making in quantity: If you are making more than 1 stocking draw an outline for each pattern on the grid fabric and do all cross-stitch at once before cutting out. In this way you'll have plenty of fabric to fit in the embroidery hoop wherever you're working on the design.

To make matching ornaments, trace the star patterns on the same fabric and work at the same time.

Initially hearts

Any cross-stitch project done on a graph or checked fabric is an easy technique because the area for each stitch is defined. The heart shape is delightfully simple, and each one can be personalized with initials or names of family and friends. You can make several as easily as one, and they can be made of one color or a combination of colors. These are done on red and white checks with white stitches. If you use white Aida or Hardanger cloth, you can create a full-color design on the white background.

Materials: small piece of grid fabric (see source list), white cotton embroidery floss, polyfill, lace trim, embroidery needle, hoop.

Directions: Trace the heart pattern shown actual size. Transfer to the fabric (see page 13), leaving enough fabric around this to fit in the embroidery hoop. This outline is the sewing line, not the cutting line. Place fabric in the embroidery hoop and follow the chart for cross-stitching.

Fold the fabric so you have a double layer and cut out the heart shape, leaving ¼-inch seam allowance all around.

With right sides facing and lace trim between, pin front and back of heart together at the edges. Stitch around the heart, leaving 2 inches open on one side. Turn right side out and press from the back. Turn open area in and press. Stuff the heart with polyfill and stitch opening closed with lace between front and back edge.

Tack a loop of ¼-inch red satin ribbon at the top for hanging. Make a small bow and tack in place as shown.

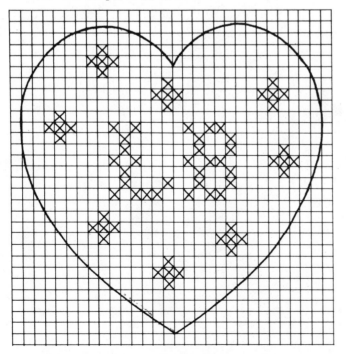

Christmas soldiers

This is the perfect stocking for any little soldier. The cross-stitch banner cuff sports stiff toy soldiers with their flags proclaiming Noel. Make it with bright colors of felt and embroidery stitches.

Materials: ¼ yard royal blue felt; 9x12-inch red felt square; 6x9-inch white Aida cloth (art needlework stores); red and black embroidery floss; embroidery hoop; needle; red, blue and white thread.

Directions: Enlarge the pattern and transfer to royal blue felt. Cut 2 pieces. Trace heel and toe pieces same size on red felt and cut 1 each. Place each piece on the front of 1 stocking piece and stitch around curved inside edge, but not the seam edges.

Place Aida in the embroidery hoop and follow the charted design for cross-stitch illustration. (See page 125 for cross-stitch.) Turn all edges of cuff under ¼ inch to back of fabric and press. Place cuff on top of front stocking piece. Stitch across top and bottom edge. Place front of stocking on back piece and stitch together at the edges.

Tack a hanging loop at side seam.

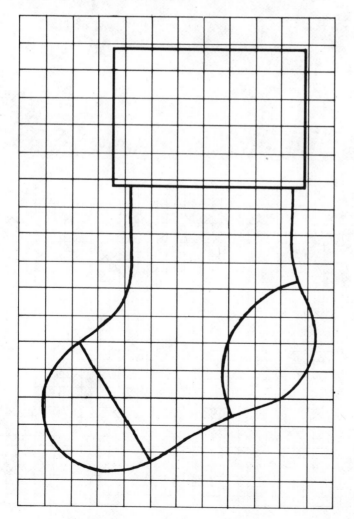

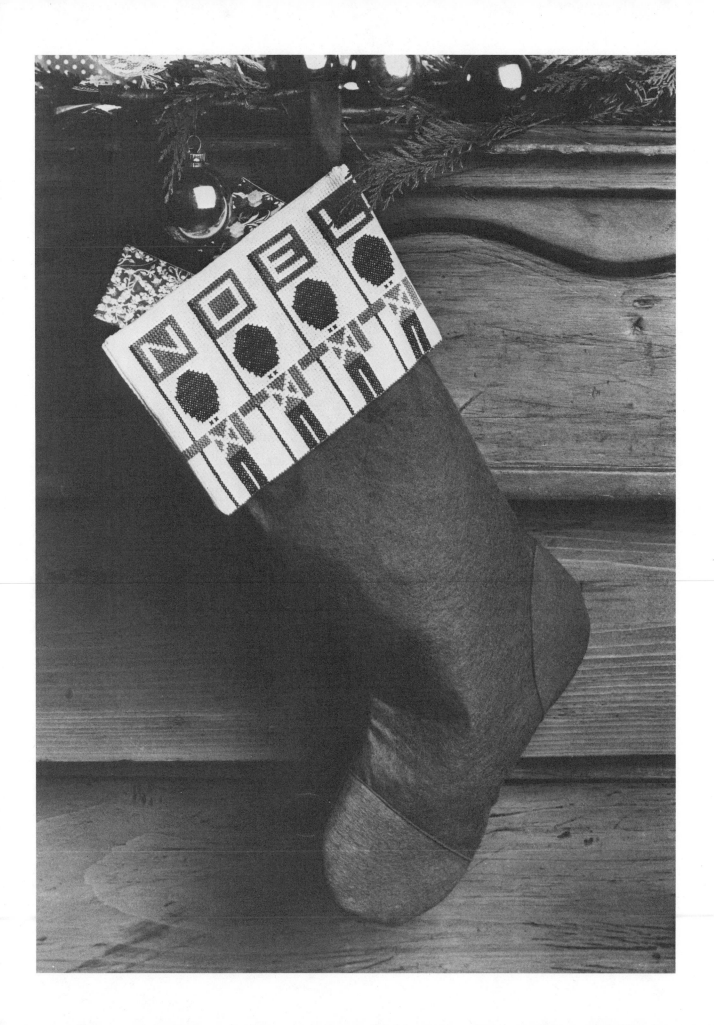

Scrap crafts

When doing any kind of craft work there are always pieces of assorted things left over. As any good crafter worth his or her stuff will tell you, nothing ever gets thrown away. Go into any home where crafting is done on any level and you will find a basket filled with scraps of fabric, tiny bits of thread, a stray button and enough yarn in every color of the rainbow to make 3 afghans (if you want 3 rainbow-colored afghans).

Being a craft writer/designer for many years, I've saved my share of scraps, and every time I design a new batch of projects for a magazine or make up 100 projects for a book, you can imagine the scraps I accumulate. Therefore I'm a sympathizer and believe that there should be some way to eliminate some, if not all, of that clutter. And in devising new ways to use the scraps, they miraculously turn from clutter to treasures. When we can fill a whole tree or make a beautiful stocking from things that have cost us nothing in out-of-pocket expense, that is an even greater joy.

The following projects use only a few of the scraps left from other projects: ribbons, buttons, bits of fabric, some lace and yarn. I'm sure you'll think of dozens more good ideas once you get going. Almost all your scraps can be used for gift tags and wrappings, and with everything costing so much, it pays to let your creative nature take over.

Those of you who enjoy doing crochet have written asking for more projects like the ones in *The Great Bazaar.* Coming up are some wonderful uses for scrap yarns to make quick and easy Christmas bells, angels and more.

Granny square jewels

This project was created by Sally George, owner of The Crochet Works in Baker, Oregon. She sent it to me with a letter in which she said, "I made these up last year when my whole family spent Christmas at my mother's and she wasn't planning on a tree. But my niece brought a small one, so we quickly made ornaments. This is my contribution and I'd like to share it with you." So from an expert, if you get in a jam or need quick decorations for a slightly bare part of a tree, you can make these in a jiffy.

Materials: acrylic 4-ply knitting worsted-weight yarn, a few yards of white, small scraps of Christmas colors,

hook: G

Gauge each motif approximately 2½ inches sq.

size: 6 inch

Jewel: Starting at center, with bright color, ch 4; join with a sl st to form circle.

Rnd 1: Ch 3 (counts as 1 dc), working into the circle, make 2 dc, * ch 2, 3dc, repeat from * twice more, ch 2, join in top of ch-3. End off (4 groups of 3dc and 4ch-2sps).

Rnd 2: With white (ch 3, 2 dc, ch2, 3dc), all in any one of the ch-2 spaces, chl, * (3dc, ch2, 3dc) all in the next ch-2 sp, ch 1, repeat from * twice more, join in top of ch-3. End off.

Tassels: Wrap white yarn approximately 12 times around a 3-inch piece of cardboard. Slip a 3-inch length of yarn under loops of yarn at one edge of cardboard; tie into a tight knot. Cut the loops at the other edge of the cardboard. Cut a length of yarn 6½ inches long and tie snugly around all strands of yarn about ½ inch down from top knot.

Pull excess tails of yarn into the center bundle. Tie tassel onto one corner of jewel with the 3-inch yarn used to tie the top knot.

Cut 4-inch length of white yarn and slip through ch-2 at corner opposite the tassel, making a hanging loop.

Sally also says that these tree ornaments can be package trims, key rings or necklaces. Furthermore, if you're caught in a pinch, as she was, you may find your checkbook is just 3 inches, perfect for winding tassels!

Making in quantity: Make all the centers you need, then do all the white rnds at one time. For "production line" tassels, wind yarn around 3-inch width until the surface is full. Slip 3-inch yarn under just 12 loops, tie and go on to another 12 loops, tie again and continue to the end. Cut all of them off at the bottom. You can do this all at one time. (For more patterns see source list.)

Patchwork stocking

Dig out all your most colorful remnants and scraps of fabric for a traditional patchwork stocking. This country classic can be made in many different styles. Patches of satin or velvet, for example, can be used to create a romantic mood, especially with a crocheted or lace cuff. If you use Christmas material or bright calico, your stocking will add to the holiday cheer. Or try a stocking from worn-out blue jeans and cover it with bright red-felt patches for a young child.

Materials: scraps of fabric, polyester batting, ½ yard solid cotton or quilted fabric for lining, 6 inches red satin ½-inch ribbon, 3 yards bias tape, cording or lace trim, ½ yard gathered eyelet trim, bells (optional).

Directions: Unfortunately it is very difficult to make a stocking pattern same size in a book (see source list for same-size patterns); therefore you will have to begin by enlarging the pattern. Transfer to lining material. Cut 2 pieces of lining and 2 pieces of batting. Baste lining to batting.

To make the patchwork design you can use irregular pieces of fabric or cut patches all the same size. If you are using 2 or 3 different fabrics, cut same-size patch squares in equal amounts from each. There are so many variations that you can create for this project that I'm sure you'll want to take the time to decide what color scheme you'd like best.

You will need 100 2-inch squares. Follow the diagram and sew fabric squares in vertical rows in the following way: 1 row of 9 squares, 3 rows of 10, 1 row of 4 and 1 row of 2. Pin the row of 9 squares right side up on the batting at the heel side edge. Place 1 row of 10 squares face down on the first strip, lining up the squares.

Stitch inside edge through all layers. Open flat and press. Continue to cover the area in this way, adding each successive strip of squares. Trim the edges, using the lining side as a pattern guide. Repeat this procedure for the back, or you can use a solid piece of fabric. Finish off top edges with double-fold bias tape.

With lining sides together, sew front to back and trim excess material from seams. Bind edges with bias tape. Stitch lace or eyelet trim around the top edge and fold back down over the stocking to form a 3-inch cuff. Fold the 6-inch ribbon in half and tack to the inside for hanging.

If you want to add a name to the cuff, you can do this with embroidery stitches (see page 44), using the alphabet on page 116. This will further personalize each stocking.

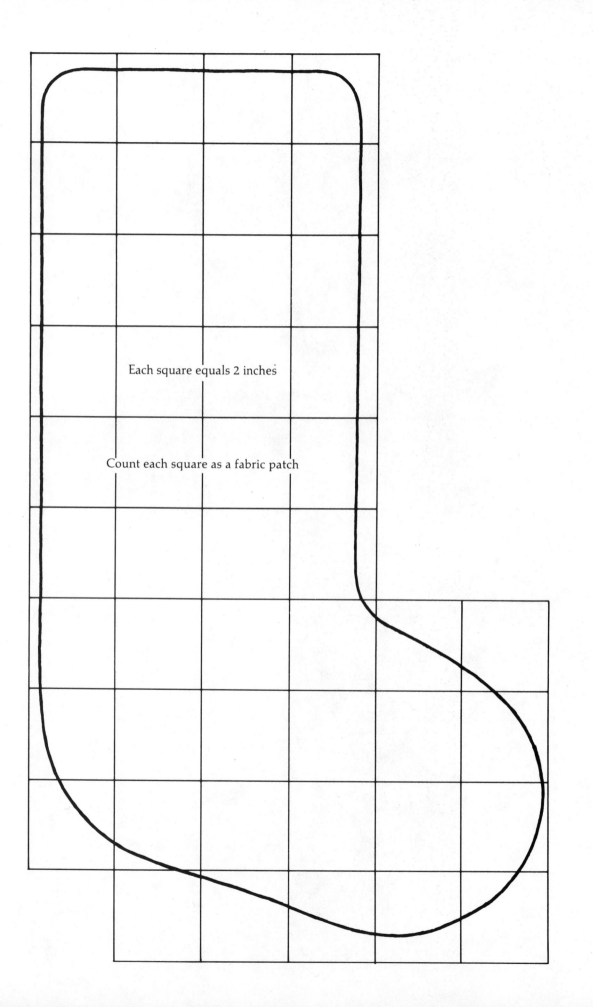

Each square equals 2 inches

Count each square as a fabric patch

Buttons and bells

Make up a stocking of buttons and bells from the vast assortment of ribbons available in your notions store. Each stocking can have the same basic design, varied for each person with the use of a different combination of ribbons. The round red buttons can be replaced by more decorative ones, like those shaped as hearts, apples, bunnies that are found in well-stocked sewing stores. Or use beads and sequins from the craft shop.

Materials: ½ yard of muslin, quilt batting, small piece of satin or taffeta for cuff, a variety of ribbons, 15 buttons per stocking, 5 bells per stocking.

Directions: Enlarge the pattern and transfer to the muslin. (See page 13.) Cut 2 pieces for the front and 2 for the back. Cut 2 pieces of batting and 2 pieces of satin for the cuff.

Sandwich the batting between layers of muslin for the front and back of the stocking. Determine placement of ribbon strips so they are evenly spaced on the front of the stocking. The buttons will go between, so leave enough space. (See diagram for placement.)

Pin back pieces to front of stocking and stitch together. Trim seams and turn inside out. With right sides together, stitch side seams of cuff to each other. Pin front raw edge of cuff to inside top edge of stocking and stitch around. Turn cuff out over the stocking and add a loop of ribbon to one side for hanging. Sew bells to the bottom edge of the finished stocking so they are evenly spaced.

Making in quantity: If you are making more than one stocking, consider different sizes. The small size shown here is perfect for the children, and a larger pattern can be used for mother and father. Choose ribbons accordingly for each design. A bold Scotch plaid for dad, pastel flowers and lace trim for mom and bright polka dots and stripes for the kids. Bells come in different sizes. Select the right size in proportion to your stocking.

Cut all muslin pieces at once. Measure and cut all ribbon strips and pin in place on each stocking. When sewing, all steps will be the same for 3, 4, 5 or whatever number stockings you are making. Do all hand-sewing of buttons and bells last. Consider hand-embroidering names on each cuff. Use the alphabet on page 112.

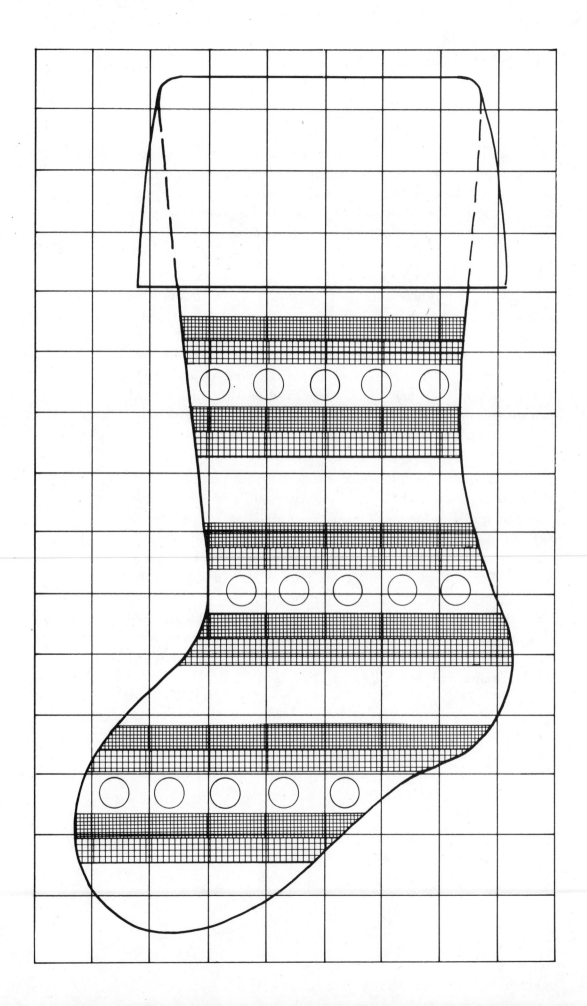

Gift tags

Many of the crafting techniques can be used to make personalized gift tags. Some of the ornament designs can be adapted in a smaller version for tags as well. Imagine adding this touch to your tree area. You might have the tree covered with paper folk ornaments, with the packages underneath sporting miniature paper folk ornaments.

Folk tags

The shapes shown here can be used same size. Cut them out from balsa wood and decorate in the following ways:

Each shape can be dyed in Rit dye (see page 101) or covered with decorative wrapping or wallpaper. Each can also be painted white, then colored with felt markers or painted with watercolors. When making these in quantity, use spray paint to coat sheet of balsa, then cut out each shape.

Gift tag reversibles

This technique is one of the fastest methods for achieving a dramatic personalized gift card. The designs and names are made by dripping rubber cement from the brush that comes in the bottle. The brush is used just like a wand.

Write a name or make a star on your gift card. Let it dry completely. Paint over the entire surface with colored ink in a bright holiday color like red, green or blue. Let the ink dry completely.

Rub the rubber cement off with your finger to reveal a bright white design under the color. The rubber cement masks the surface from the color. Try various designs shown or make up your own. Names and initials are always appreciated.

Crochet

For those of you who enjoy making crocheted projects I've solicited the help of two designers in this field to share their Christmas creations. Anne Lane of Anne Lane Originals and Sally George of The Crochet Works have worked out the patterns for some of the most popular decorations. These include snowflakes to cover your tree and a darling angel to top it off as well as a reindeer, a gingerbread house with boy and girl hand puppets, and a wonderful granny-square stocking complete with mouse toe. All of these projects can be made from scrap yarns and even a beginner will find the directions easy to follow.

The abbreviations that follow can be referred to when doing each of the projects. ch = chain; dc = double crochet; dec = decrease; " = inches; jn = join; lp = loop; oz = ounce; rnd = round; sc = single crochet; sk = skip; sl st = slip stitch; st = stitch; sp = space; thru = through; tr = triple; yo = yarn over hook. To decrease in single crochet, draw up a loop in each of the next two stitches, yarn over hook and through all 3 loops on hook.

Little angel

Who could resist putting our little angel on the top of the tree? However, if your family is set on the traditional star Sally George's angel comes complete with halo and hanging loop to hang her anywhere. This is one of four that can be made quickly, easily and inexpensively. You might consider placing some angel hair (sold in boxes along with tinsel, etc.) on the branch under the angel. Place one of the tree lights under the fluffy angel's hair and another light under your crocheted angel's head for a special effect.

Materials: 4-ply knitting worsted weight yarn, few ozs. each of pale pink for head and arms, yellow for halo and wings, brown or yellow for hair, white for trim, any color for the dress, blue or brown yarn for the eyes and a bit of red embroidery floss for the mouth, small amount of polyfill, yarn needle, G and an H hook.

Gauge: 4 sc = 1 inch
            4 rows sc = 1 inch

Directions

Head

Starting at top, with G hook and pink yarn, ch 2.

Rnd 1: 6 sc in 2nd ch from hook. Do not join with sl st but work in continuous spiral, marking rnds with contrasting color yarn.

Rnd 2: 2 sc in ea sc. (12 sc)

Rnd 3: (1 sc in next sc, 2 sc in next sc) 6 times. (18 sc)

Next 3 rnds- 4, 5 & 6: sc in ea sc. Begin stuffing with polyfill.

Rnd 7: (1 sc in next sc, 1 dec in next 2 sc) 6 times. Finish stuffing with polyfill. (12 sc)

Rnd 8: (dec in next 2 sc) 6 times, sl st to next sc. End off.

Arms (Make 2):

With G hook and pink, ch 8. Sc in 2nd ch from hook and ea of next 5 ch, 3 sc in end ch; working along opposite side of ch, sc in ea ch. End off, leaving 6" yarn for sewing. Fold piece in half lengthwise and sew sides together with overcast sts, catching the outside loops. By pulling the sts slightly, you can make the arm curve. If you'd like bendable arms, put a pipe cleaner in before sewing.

Halo

With G hook and yellow, ch 25 tightly (or 5 inches), join. End off leaving 3" yarn for sewing.

Wings (Make 2):

With G hook and yellow, ch 10.

Row 1: sl st in 2nd ch from hook, 2 sc in next ch, dc in next ch, holding back last loop of ea st, dc in ea of next 4 ch (5 loops on hook), yo and thru all 5 loops, dc in next ch, 2 dc in last ch. End off, leaving 5" for

sewing.

Dress

With G hook and color of choice, starting at top, ch 8, join with sl st to form ring.

Note—When working rnds in sc that are joined with a sl st, always work the first sc into the same sc that is sl-st'd into (also called the joining st). In this way, at the end of ea rnd, all the sl sts line up on top of ea other and are not counted nor worked into.

Rnd 1: (ch 5, sl st in next ch) 7 times, ch 3, dc in last ch. (8 lps)

Rnd 2: (ch 3, sl st in 3rd ch of next ch-5 lp) 7 times, ch 3, sl st in dc to join. (8 lps)

Rnd 3: sl st in each of next ch, (ch 1, 4 dc in 2nd ch of next ch-3 lp, ch 1, sl st in 2nd ch of next ch-3 lp for shell) 4 times, join to 2nd sl st made before first ch-1. (4 shells)

Rnd 4: ch 1, sc in joining st, * 2 sc in ch-1, 2 sc in each of next 4 dc, 2 sc in ch-1, sc in sl st, skip next shell to make sleeve, sc in sl st, repeat from * once more, join to first sc, ch 1. (28 sc)

Next 5 rnds— 5 thru 9: change to H hook, sc in ea sc, join, ch 1. At end of Rnd 9, end off main color.

Rnd 10: with white, * ch 1, sk 1 sc, (dc, ch 1) 3 times in next sc, sk next sc, sl st in next sc, repeat from * around, join. End off.

Finishing

With dress yarn, sew head to neck of dress. Push arms up into sleeves and sew in place with dress yarn. With yellow, sew wings in place with flat edge of wings on chs just above shell. They will touch at the top but spread apart at the bottom. Hairstyles: Thread yarn needle so strand of 6 yarn is double. Following the illustration, take long stitches from one side of head (A) to other side (C), going under an sc loop at top center of head (B) where the part would be. Continue in this manner until entire head is covered.

Features: Keep it simple. Use French knots in yarn for eyes or sew on a small sequin. Use stem stitch with floss for mouth (will only take 2 or 3 sts). Sally doesn't bother with a mouth. She finds it looks like smeared lipstick.

Place halo on top of hair with sl st at back; tack in that place only so the halo will float over the head.

Make a hanging loop out of sewing thread and attach to top of head.

Crochet snowflakes

When researching those projects that sell best at fairs and bazaars across the country, I found Sally George of The Crochet Works. She has sold patterns for hundreds of crocheted snowflakes and her customers can't make enough of them. When Sally last wrote to me she said that each snowflake can take up to 48 pins and her fingers were sore from making them, but they are worth the effort. When a tree is covered with a variety of snowflake patterns in different sizes it takes on a romantic quality. Fill your tree with stiffened snowflakes or use them with others that you might choose. And then make a one-of-a-kind crocheted angel to watch over all at the top of the tree.

These are just three patterns of the many offered in Sally's catalog of patterns. If you want to make more, write to her for a list of the other designs. (See Source List.)

Materials: Knit-Cro-Sheen and a #6 steel hook.

Snowflake A—(Approximately 3¼ inches across.)

Starting at center, ch 6, join with sl st to form ring.

Rnd 1: ch 3, into ring work 1 dc, ch 1, * 2 dc, ch 1, repeat from * 4 times, join to top of ch-3.

Rnd 2: ch 3, 1 dc in same st, 2 dc in next dc, ch 1, * 2 dc in ea of next 2 dc, ch 1, repeat from * around, join to top of ch-3.

Rnd 3: ** ch 5, work 1 tr loosely in 3rd dc in group of 4 made in previous rnd, ch 4, sl st in top of tr, ch 5, sk next dc, sl st in ch-1 sp, * ch 4, sl st in 4th ch from hook, repeat from * twice, sl st in same ch-1 sp, repeat from ** around, join. End off.

Snowflake B—(Approximately 4¾ inches across.)

Starting at center, ch 6, join with sl st to form ring.

Rnd 1: ch 1, 12 sc into ring, join.

Rnd 2: ch 5, * dc in next sc, ch 2, repeat from * around, join to 3rd ch of ch-5.

Rnd 3: ch 10, sc in 2nd ch from hook, dc in ea of next 8 ch (petal made), sl st in next dc, (ch 7, sl st into sp) twice, ch 7, sl st in next dc, repeat from * around, ending with a ch 4, dc into last sp.

Rnd 4: * sc in 4th ch and ea of next 5 ch along side of petal, sl st in ch at tip of petal, (ch 4, sl st in 4th ch from hook for picot) 3 times, sl st in same st at tip of petal, sc in each of next 6 sts along other side of petal, ch, 1, sc into top of first ch-7 loop, ch 1, sc into top of next loop, ch 3, sl st into sc just made, ch 1, sc into next loop, ch 1, repeat from * around, join. End off.

Snowflake C—(Approximately 5½ inches across.)

Starting at center, ch 4, join with sl st to form ring, ch 3.

Rnd 1: work 11 dc into ring, join in top of ch-3.

Rnd 2: ch 3, dc in same st, ch 2, sk 1 dc, * 2 dc in next dc, ch 2, sk 1 dc, repeat from * 4 times, join at top of ch-3, ch 3.

Rnd 3: 2 dc in next dc, ch 4, * 1 dc in next dc, 2 dc in next dc, ch 4, repeat from * around, join, ch 3.

Rnd 4: 2 dc in next dc, 1 dc in next dc, ch 5, * dc in next dc, 2 dc in next dc, 1 dc in next dc, ch 5, repeat from * around, join.

Rnd 5: *ch 3, sl st in next dc, ch 5, sl st in 4th ch from hook for picot, ch 2, sl st in next dc, ch 3, sl st in next dc, (ch 6, sl st in 4th ch from hook for picot) 3 times, ch 2, dc into base of 2nd picot from hook, ch 4, sl st into top of dc just made, ch 2, tr into base of next picot, ch 4, sl st into tr just made, ch 2, sl st in next dc, repeat from * around, join. End off.

Starching and Blocking

Materials: sheet of styrofoam, typing paper, plastic wrap, masking tape, box of rustproof copper pins, paper towels, waterproof pen, your choice of stiffening agents as listed below:

Stif'n Fab—Available in craft stores or directly from dealer. (See Source List.) Shake, pour in a small bowl and soak snowflakes. Dries rapidly. Water soluble for easy clean up and future laundering.

Dry Starch—mix and cook a heavy solution as directed on the box. Allow to cool. Pre-mixed liquid and spray starches don't give enough body.

Sugar—heat ½ cup water with ¾ cup sugar until sugar dissolves. Allow to cool.

Directions: With waterproof pen, draw the pattern on the typing paper (approximately 6 per sheet) and tape the paper to the styrofoam sheet. Cover all with plastic wrap and tape in place. Soak snowflakes in stiffening agent; squeeze out excess, blotting between paper towels if necessary; place on pattern, matching centers. Pin outside points along pattern lines. Then repin, stretching opposite points against each other. Finish by pinning each picot and each loop. Allow to dry.

Make a loop of fine thread or monofilament line and tie for hanging.

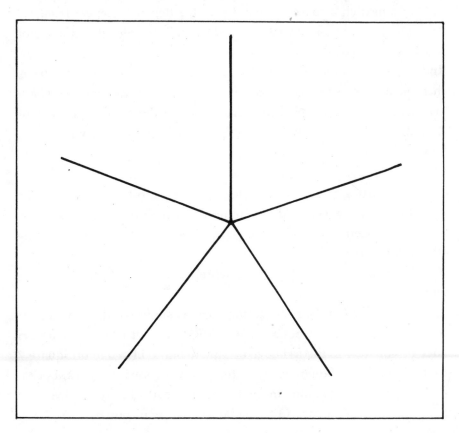

Mouse stocking

Imagine your child's excitement over this mouse toe stocking. Made of thirteen easy-to-crochet granny squares, this Christmas project will be treasured for years. You can use scraps of yarn and make each square a different color, or you can do as Anne Lane has done with hers, making each square with red, green and white yarn. The mouse face is gray with adorable pink ears and nose. Anne's other designs include a Santa face or loopy dog. After making the design presented here you'll surely be hooked. (See Source List.)

Materials: 3 oz. red knitting worsted (Color A), 1½ oz. white knitting worsted (Color B), 1 oz. green knitting worsted (Color C), 1 oz. gray knitting worsted, size H crochet hook, size F crochet hook, 2 black beads or shank buttons, small scrap of pink felt, waxed white carpet thread, yarn needle.

Granny Square Pattern (Make 13)

Working with size H crochet hook and Color C ch 4; jn with a sl st to form ring.

Rnd 1: Ch 3 (to count as dc), make 2 dc in ring; ch 2. * Make 3 dc in ring; ch 2. Repeat from * 2 times (12 dc). Jn to top of ch 3 with a sl st. End off Color C and jn Color B to any ch 2 space.

Rnd 2: Ch 3 (to count as dc), make 2 dc, ch 2, make 3 dc in same space; ch 1. * In next ch 2 space make 3 dc, ch 2, 3 dc; ch 1. Repeat from * 2 times (24 dc). Jn to top of ch 3 with a sl st. End off Color B and jn Color A to any ch 2 space.

Rnd 3: Ch 3 (to count as dc), make 2 dc, ch 2, make 3 dc in same space, ch 1, make 3 dc in the ch 1 space of RND 2; ch 1. * In next ch 2 space make 3 dc, ch 2, 3 dc; ch 1 and make 3 dc in the next ch 1 space of RND 2; ch 1. Repeat from * 2 times (36 dc). Jn to top of ch 3 with a sl st. End off Color A.

Granny Square Assembly

Before starting to sew squares together, refer to the diagram at the end of this section as an aid in determining where the squares go. Sew all squares together with Color A yarn and neat overcast stitches, using the *back lps of rnd 3 only.*

1. Sew Squares 1-3 together in a row; repeat this for Squares 4-6, 7-9 and 10-12.

2. Sew the rows together, staggering them as shown in the diagram.

3. Sew the LH edge of Square 1 to the RH edge of Square 3; the LH edge of Square 4 to the RH edge of Square 6; the LH edge of Square 7 to the RH edge of Square 9. Leave the last row (Squares 10-12) open.

4. Sew any gaps remaining in the horizontal seams between rows.

5. Sew 3 edges of Square 13 to the bottom edges of Squares 10-12.

Top Border and Hanging Loop

Jn white yarn to top of stocking.

Rnd 1: Working with a Size H hook, sc around top of stocking. At end of this rnd ch 12; jn last ch to first ch of rnd with a sl st.

Rnd 2: sc around top of stocking and over 12 sc of LOOP.

Rnd 3: sc around top of stocking. End off.

The "granny square" portion of the stocking is now complete; you are ready to go on to the "stocking pet" part.

Mouse Head

Working with Size F hook and gray yarn, ch 2.

Rnd 1: Make 6 sc in 2nd. ch from hook. Do not jn rnds; carry a piece of contrasting color yarn between first and last sc to mark beginning of rnds.

Rnd 2: Work even on 6 sc.

Rnd 3: Inc in each sc around (12 sc).

Rnd 4: Work even on 12 sc.

Rnds 5-8: Inc 6 sc evenly spaced in each rnd (36 sc in 8th. rnd).

Rnds 9-15: Work even on 36 sc. At end of rnd 15 end off gray yarn and jn red yarn.

Rnds 16-18: Work even on 36 sc. End off at end of rnd 18.

Mouse Ears (Make 2)

Working with Size F hook and gray yarn, ch 2.

Row 1: Make 5 sc in 2nd ch from hook. Ch 1 and turn.

Row 2; sc in first sc, inc over each of next 3 sc, sc in last sc (8 sc). Ch 1 and turn.

Row 3: sc in first 3 sc, inc over each of next 2 sc, sc in last 3 sc (10 sc). End off.

Finishing

1. Sew *head* to bottom of stocking.

2. Sew 2 black heads or shank buttons to face for eyes.

3. Cut a small circle from scrap of pink felt; sew it to tip of nose.

4. Cut ear linings from scrap of pink felt and sew them to insides of *ears;* and sew *ears* to top of *head* on either side.

5. Run a doubled strand of waxed white carpet thread through the face several times about 2 sc back from tip of nose. Trim to the desired length for whiskers.

Granny square assembly diagram

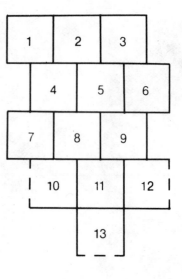

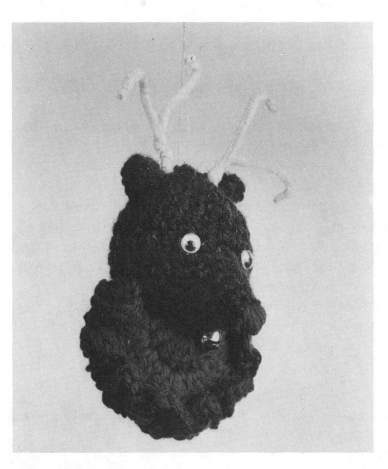

Reindeer ornament

Make all of Santa's reindeer from scraps of yarn and add pipe cleaner antlers. Another of Anne Lane's Originals, the reindeer is one of a group of snowmen, santas and angels, but this is my favorite and I'm sure you'll enjoy making it as well.

Materials: ½ oz. spice brown knitting worsted, ½ oz. red knitting worsted, ½ oz. green knitting worsted, 2″ styrofoam ball, 2 black beads, for eyes or ¼″ wiggle eyes, 2 white or brown 6″ pipe cleaners, 1 small bell, small amount of stuffing for nose, 12″ of gold cord, Size F crochet hook, yarn needle.

Head
Starting at top of head, with spice brown yarn ch 2.
Rnd 1: Make 6 sc in 2nd ch from hook. Do not jn rnds; carry a piece of contrasting color yarn between first and last sc to mark beginning of rnds.
Rnd 2: Inc in each sc around (12 sc).
Rnd 3: * Sc in 1st sc, inc in next sc. Repeat from * around (18 sc).
Rnd 4: * Sc in first 2 sc, inc in next sc. Repeat from * around (24 sc).
Rnds 5-10: Work even on 24 sc.
Rnd 11: * Sc in first 2 sc, dec over next sc. Repeat from * around (18 sc).

Rnd 12: Insert styrofoam ball. Working around ball, * sc in 1st, sc, dec over next 2 sc. Repeat from * around (12 sc).

Rnd 13: Dec 6 sc evenly spaced around (6 sc).

Rnd 14: Work even on 6 sc. End off spice brown yarn and jn red yarn.

Rnd 15: Ch 3 (to count as dc), in 1st. sc make 2 dc. In next sc and each sc around make 3 dc. Jn last dc to top of ch 3 with a sl st (18 dc).

Rnd 16: Ch 3 (to count as dc), in 1st dc make a dc. In next dc and each dc around make 2 dc. Jn last dc to top of ch 3 with a sl st (36 dc). End off red yarn and jn green yarn.

Rnd 17: *(Work in back lps only)* Make 3 dc in each dc around (18 dc). End off, leaving a 12" length of yarn for sewing. Fold "body" in half and stitch firmly through RND 16.

Nose

Starting at tip of nose, with spice brown yarn ch 2.

Rnd 1: Make 6 sc in 2nd ch from hook. Do not jn rnds; mark as for head.

Rnd 2: Work even on 6 sc.

Rnd 3: Inc 3 sc evenly spaced around (9 sc).

Rnd 4: Work even on 9 sc.

Rnd 5: Inc 3 sc evenly spaced around (12 sc). End off, leaving a 12" length of yarn for sewing nose to head.

Ears (Make 2)

With spice brown yarn ch 5.

Row 1: sc in 2nd, 3rd and 4th ch from hook, 3 sc in last ch. Working in opposite side of starting ch sc in 3 spaces. End off, leaving a 6 " length of yarn for sewing ear to head.

Finishing

1. Stuff nose firmly and sew to head. With red yarn make several stitches at tip of nose.

2. Sew black beads in position for eyes, or glue on wiggle eyes.

3. Tie the small bell around the neck with a short length of green yarn.

4. Sew an ear to either side of head at the top.

5. Working at top of head, run a pipe cleaner underneath crocheted surface but outside of styrofoam ball, starting slightly in front of one ear and emerging slightly in front of the other. Leave 1½" sticking out on one side and 2½" on the other. Now repeat this with the other pipe cleaner, but reverse the lengths left sticking out on each side. Bend all four tips up so they are vertical, then bend last ½" of each tip outward.

6. Run the length of gold cord through the top of the head and tie a loop, for hanging ornament on the tree.

Gingerbread puppets and house

The gingerbread house is actually a little pouch that hangs as an ornament and can later become a child's purse. You might like to crochet a shoulder strap to attach or use the loop to hang on a belt. The surprise in this ornament is the crocheted gingerbread boy and girl that become finger puppets. This is a project that will delight any child after the other ornaments have been packed away.

Materials: 1 oz. brown knitting worsted, ½ oz. white knitting worsted, small amounts of pink and green knitting worsted, size F crochet hook, yarn needle, 4¼"-diameter wiggle eyes.

House (Make 2)

Working with brown yarn, ch 16.

Row 1: sc in 2nd ch from hook and in remaining 14 ch (15 sc). Ch 1 and turn.

Rows 2-12: Work even on 15 sc. Ch 1 and turn at end of each row.

Row 13: *(Roof shaping begins)* Dec over first sc, sc in 11 sc, dec over last 2 sc (13 sc). Ch 1 and turn.

Rows 14-18: Dec 1 sc at beginning *and* end of each row (3 sc on ROW 18). Ch 1 and turn at end of each row.

Row 19: Pull up a loop in each of the remaining 3 sc, yo and through all lps on hook. End off. With white yarn, starting at ROW 12 and working Side-Bottom-Side-Roof, sc around entire house. End off, leaving a 16" length of yarn for sewing.

Handle

Working with brown yarn, ch 3.

Row 1: sc in 2nd ch from hook and in last ch (2 sc). Ch 1 and turn.

Rows 2-24: Work even on 2 sc. Ch 1 and turn at end of each row, *except* at the end of ROW 24 end off.

Assembly

1. With white yarn, sew sides and bottom of house together using a neat overcast stitch.

2. With white yarn, blanket stitch across ROW 11 of one house for trim.

3. Working on front of *puppet pouch,* with white yarn outline windows and door in chain stitch.

4. With scraps of green and pink yarn, embroider flowers underneath windows.

5. Sew an end of the *handle* to each roof peak, working on inside of *puppet pouch.*

Gingerbread boy and girl pattern (Makes 2)

With brown yarn, ch 2.

Rnd 1: Make 6 sc in 2nd ch from hook. Do not jn rnds; carry a piece of contrasting color yarn between first and last sc to mark beginning of rnds.

Rnd 2: Inc in each sc around (12 sc).

Rnds 3-12: Work even on 12 sc. End off at end of RND 12.

Finishing

Gingerbread boy

1. Glue eyes to head.

2. With scraps of white yarn, embroider a smiling mouth and two

"buttons" on front.

3. With white yarn, make a small pom-pom for hair. Trim to create a fuzzy look.

Gingerbread girl

1. Glue eyes to head.

2. With scraps of white yarn, embroider a smiling mouth and two "buttons" on front.

3. For hair, cut 20 6-inch-long pieces of white yarn. Sew to top of head with a back stitch; catch at sides of head with bow ties of white yarn. Trim where necessary.

Source List

Most of the supplies used for the projects in the book are familiar and can be found in most variety, fabric or hobby shops. However, I have listed a few sources for those specific items that may be difficult to locate and which can be purchased through mail order. If you have trouble with any project or can't locate materials write to me and I will send you a source.

Aida cloth, Hardanger cloth and plastic canvas

American Cross Stitch
P.O. Box 4235
Parkersburg, WV 26101

Enterprise Art
2860 Roosevelt Blvd.
Clearwater, FL 33520

Colored plastic canvas

The Farm
Box 446
Manchester, MD 21102

Crochet patterns

Anne Lane Originals
P.O. Box 206
North Abington, MA 02351

The Crochet Works
1472 Auburn
Baker, OR 97814
catalog 25¢

Crochet stiffener for snowflakes

Posi Bendr
P.O. Box 2173
Westminister, CA 92683

Fom-Cor

Charrette
31 Olympia Ave.
Woburn, MA 01801
catalog $1

Felt

Commonwealth Felt Co.
211 Congress St.
Boston, MA 02110

Grid fabric

Fabrications
146 E. 56th St.
New York, N.Y. 10022

Full-size patterns

If you would like to receive full-size patterns for those projects that must be enlarged send a stamped self addressed envelope to:

Leslie Linsley Enterprises
Main St.
Nantucket, MA 02554

Please specify name of project and book page number.